At Issue

Does the World Hate the US?

Other Books in the At Issue Series:

At Issue

Does the World Hate the US?

Noah Berlatsky, Book Editor

GREENHAVEN PRESS
A part of Gale, Cengage Learning

 GALE
CENGAGE Learning·

Detroit • New York • San Francisco • New Haven, Conn • Waterville, Maine • London

Elizabeth Des Chenes, *Director, Publishing Solutions*

© 2013 Greenhaven Press, a part of Gale, Cengage Learning.

Gale and Greenhaven Press are registered trademarks used herein under license.

For more information, contact:
Greenhaven Press
27500 Drake Rd.
Farmington Hills, MI 48331-3535
Or you can visit our Internet site at gale.cengage.com

For product information and technology assistance, contact us at

Gale Customer Support, 1-800-877-4253
For permission to use material from this text or product, submit all requests online at www.cengage.com/permissions

Further permissions questions can be e-mailed to permissionrequest@cengage.com

Articles in Greenhaven Press anthologies are often edited for length to meet page requirements. In addition, original titles of these works are changed to clearly present the main thesis and to explicitly indicate the author's opinion. Every effort is made to ensure that Greenhaven Press accurately reflects the original intent of the authors. Every effort has been made to trace the owners of copyrighted material.

Cover image © Images.com/Corbis.

LIBRARY OF CONGRESS CATALOGING-IN-PUBLICATION DATA

Does the world hate the US? / Noah Berlatsky, book editor.
    p. cm. -- (At issue)
    Includes bibliographical references and index.
    ISBN 978-0-7377-6171-9 (hbk.) -- ISBN 978-0-7377-6172-6 (pbk.)
    1. Anti-Americanism. 2. United States--Foreign public opinion. 3. United States--Foreign relations--2001-2009. 4. United States--Relations. 5. Civilization, Modern--American influences. I. Berlatsky, Noah.
    E895.D642 2012
    327.73--dc23
                                                                    2012025801

Printed in the United States of America
1 2 3 4 5 6 7 16 15 14 13 12

Contents

Introduction

Russia has had a long history of conflict with the United States. For four decades after World War II, Russia was the heart of the Soviet Union, a Communist state that engaged in a so-called Cold War with America. In the Cold War, the Soviet Union and the US attempted to advance their influence and power in the world by aggressive means without ever engaging in all-out war.

The Soviet Union collapsed in 1991. Following the end of Communism, Russia, encouraged by America and the West, embraced democracy and capitalism. Under Communism, the state had attempted to control most economic activity and owned many industries. Under capitalism, state properties were sold off and individuals were encouraged to become business owners and entrepreneurs. At that point, relations between America and Russia were much improved.

The Russian transition to capitalism was rocky. There was massive corruption and a severe economic contraction, leading to high rates of poverty as the Communist welfare system was dismantled. Rajon Menon, writing in an August 20, 2006 article for the *New America Foundation* says that as Russians became disenchanted with capitalism, they also became disenchanted with America. Menon quotes one Russian official who told him, "We followed your advice, and look where it landed us."

Russian anti-Americanism is not just based in past grievances, however. The two countries also have many policy differences that cause tensions. Russia, like many nations throughout the world, resents what it regards as the assertive use of American military might in places like Iraq and Afghanistan. Russia has also opposed the expansion of NATO, a European-American alliance originally created to contain the Soviet Union. After the Soviet Union collapsed, NATO expanded to include former Soviet republics over which Russia once had great influence. Russia was "insulted and threatened" by these moves, according to Megan K. Stack writing in a July 4, 2009 article in the *Los Angeles Times*. More recently, Russia has come into conflict with America over Syria. The US supported a UN resolution calling for the resignation of authoritarian Syrian leader Bashar al-Assad. Russia, which is an ally of Syria's, vetoed the resolution.

Not all agree that Russian anti-Americanism is broad-based or that it is strongly linked to policy differences. On the contrary, sociology professor Vladimir Shlapentokh argues in an October 5, 2009 *New York Times* article that anti-American sentiment in Russia is not a popular movement. Rather, he says that anti-Americanism is imposed from above. Following the 1990s, Russia moved towards a more authoritarian government, dominated by Vladimir Putin, who has served as both President and Prime Minister. Shlapentokh contends that "under Vladimir Putin, xenophobia has been restored as a leading element of the official ideology. . . . The animosity toward the United States is fomented by Russia's leaders primarily for domestic consumption—to sustain and cultivate the image of Russia as a besieged fortress and of Putin as the savior of the country." Shlapentokh concludes that without government prodding, Russian anti-Americanism would quickly evaporate.

Whether Russia's distrust of America is caused by long-standing grievances or by government propaganda, there is little doubt that it exists. A poll by Pew Global Attitudes Project found that Russia's favorability ratings of the US were consistently low. In 2007, only 41% of Russians had a favorable view of the US. In 2008, that crept upward to 46% and in 2009 it fell slightly to 44%. When asked whether the new US President, Barack Obama, would do the right thing in world affairs, only 37% of Russians thought that he would. This figure seems dismal, but it is substantially higher than the rating enjoyed by Obama's predecessor, George W. Bush. Only 22% of Russians—less than 1 in 4—believed Bush would do the right thing in world affairs.

Despite Russia's skepticism about America, however, the two countries have been successful in improving relations in some areas over the past few years. For instance, Russia has agreed to help the US in placing sanctions on Iran in an effort to dissuade that country from pursuing nuclear weapons technology. There has also been increased military cooperation between Russia and the US, with Russia participating in NATO naval training exercises near Spain in the fall of 2011. Samuel Charap, an expert on Russia at the progressive Center for American Progress, has argued that such steps are "concrete achievements for U.S. national security," as quoted in a September 14, 2011 article by Alan Greenblatt for *NPR*.

The commentators featured in *At Issue: Does the World Hate the US?* examine issues surrounding the causes and consequences of anti-American sentiment in other parts of the world—and even within the United States itself.

1

The World Hates the US Because America Is a Militaristic Empire

David Hilfiker

David Hilfiker is a physician and founder of Joseph's House, a home and hospice for homeless men and women with AIDS or cancer. His most recent book is Urban Injustice: How Ghettos Happen.

People throughout the world hate and resent the United States. This is because the United States has often acted aggressively, and uses military force and violence to achieve its goals. The United States is highly militarized; it spends huge amounts on its armed forces, and frequently resorts to military solutions. Eventually, this militarization will bankrupt and destroy the United States. To regain the respect of the world, and to ensure its own longterm health, the United States must cut defense spending and cease to engage in offensive military action.

Shortly after the attacks of 9/11, many American voices raised the question, "Why do they hate us?" The "they," in this case, was Muslim fundamentalists, but the same question could have been asked of South American peasants, of the people of Iraq or Iran, of the poor of India or Indonesia, or, indeed, of the poor anywhere.

In fact, "they" don't only hate us; the feelings of people around the world toward the United States are a complex mixture of positive and negative. On the one hand, for instance, much of the rest of the world is excited by the election [in 2008] of [U.S. president] Barack Obama. Almost six years ago [2003], visiting Iraq just before the American invasion, I listened to Iraqis who professed their admiration for much of America and how American democracy has been a "beacon" to the rest of the world. On the other hand, those same Iraqis felt betrayed by the United States that would attack a country that did not threaten it. And by 2008, multiple polls of people around the world revealed a deep anger toward our country: Clear majorities believe us to be the "greatest danger to world peace." My own coming to understand why they hate us has been a painful process, but one I consider important to share with any American who still does not understand.

My Own Conditioning: The City upon a Hill

I grew up in the 1950s. Americans were still celebrating our critical role in defeating Germany and Japan [in World War II] and, we thought, protecting the world from fascism. Our economy was as big as the combined economies of the rest of the world put together, and we had used some of that economic power through the Marshall Plan to successfully rebuild the economies of war-shattered Europe. We were the rising empire, and we saw ourselves as the world's savior. It seemed to us (middle-class whites) a time of prosperity and suburbanization, an era of magnanimity and cooperation, a period of confidence that our national path would be continuously upward. I remember predictions that our increasing economic productivity would enable us to halve the work week within a generation while still raising our standard of living.

As a society, however, we generally chose not to see the more ominous realities. Few of us reflected upon the wanton destruction of innocent life in Hiroshima and Nagasaki [Japanese cities on which the U.S. dropped atomic bombs]. The CIA-instigated overthrow of democratically elected leaders in Iran, Guatemala and elsewhere and, a little later, the assassination attempts on Fidel Castro [leader of Cuba] were only outlandish rumors (that only "the paranoid" believed). The white majority could still ignore segregation. I did not find out about the bizarre, anti-communist antics of Sen. Joe McCarthy [who accused many people of being Communist agents] until I was in college, a decade later.

Little of our dark side entered my consciousness in the 1950s and early 1960s. Rather, I grew up with the unarticulated sense that our nation was nearing the perfect society; we were "almost there," not so distant from the Kingdom of God. In Puritan Christian terminology, we were the "city upon a hill," "the light of the world" that should not be hidden. God had blessed us; we saw ourselves as exceptional people and exceptionally righteous. In 1963, I hitchhiked from London through Europe to Finland to visit my future wife, and I do not remember feeling surprised that the American flag on my luggage made it easier to get rides. Of course foreigners loved Americans; who wouldn't?

Not until much later did I make the connections between the killing of 2 million to 3 million Vietnamese. . .with the genocide of Native Americans or the enslavement of African Americans.

Vietnam, Genocide, and Slavery

Paradoxically, even the moral and political disaster of the Vietnam War reinforced my sense that America would continue to move toward its ideal. I came of age during the war and joined in active opposition to it, ultimately refusing induction into the Army. While still in college, I became a speaker for the War Resisters League, touring campuses and lecturing against the war. I learned about some of the disturbing realities of American imperialism in Southeast Asia, of course, but—again without articulating it to myself—I judged it a momentary anomaly of, rather than a continuation of, our history.

Not until much later did I make the connections between the killing of 2 million to 3 million Vietnamese (the vast majority innocent civilians) with the genocide of Native Americans or the enslavement of African Americans or the deaths of the half-million Filipino civilians who died following our 1898 attempt to control their country. Rather, I interpreted the strength of our anti-war protests to block the re-election of President Johnson and ultimately force withdrawal from Vietnam as manifestation of the power and hope of American democracy. Despite the fact that a few years later during my second trip to Europe I was better off hitchhiking *without* the American flag, the Vietnam War and our resistance to it strengthened my faith in our country, its democracy and its inherent goodness.

During the 1970s and early 1980s, I was immersed in medical school and doctoring in a small town in northern Minnesota. The war in Vietnam was over, I was not paying much attention to foreign affairs, and I was completely unaware of American interventions in Central and South America (such as the CIA participation in the overthrow of the democratically elected [Salvador] Allende government in Chile). From my point of view, American society seemed to work pretty well. We were still the city upon a hill. . . .

The Iraq Sanctions

But it was the personal confrontation with the economic sanctions imposed by the United States on Iraq that broke through my own reluctance and brought me face-to-face with the evil embedded in American political and military might.

In December 2002, shortly before the [George W.] Bush administration's invasion of Iraq, I visited the country for three weeks, out of a desire as an American to be in solidarity with a people soon to be attacked by my government. I had no particular agenda ahead of time, but I quickly learned about the United Nations economic sanctions that had been responsible for the deaths of hundreds of thousands of Iraqi children in the preceding 10 years. I also discovered that although these sanctions were officially imposed by the United Nations, they had been sustained entirely at the insistence of the United States. How could my country be responsible for the deaths of so many children?

In August 1990, after a decade of tacit (and sometimes very active) support by the United States, Saddam Hussein invaded neighboring Kuwait, an action that was universally condemned around the world. In response, under the leadership of the United States government, the United Nations Security Council authorized severe economic sanctions upon Iraq (U.N. Resolution 661) in an effort to force Saddam to withdraw from Kuwait. These were perhaps the most stringent sanctions ever imposed upon a modern nation, so severe that they could only humanely be used as *short-term* overwhelming pressure to compel withdrawal from Kuwait. It was widely appreciated by experts—even within our own government—that any long-term application of this level of economic sanctions would cause lethal civilian consequences, especially for children.

Despite the sanctions, the Iraqi army continued its occupation of Kuwait, so in January 1991, the United States led a coalition of nations in a military attack on Iraqi occupation troops in Kuwait, forcing a hasty retreat. While the military power of the United States and its allies easily overpowered Iraqi forces, the coalition decided for political reasons only to repel the Iraq invasion of Kuwait and attack Iraq by air but not to invade Iraq with ground troops or use military force to remove Saddam completely from power. But during the six-week air war, the Iraqi military had been decimated, including the complete destruction of the air force. The civilian infrastructure of Iraq—including electrical generation, sanitation and water purification—had been profoundly damaged.

The Iraqi withdrawal from Kuwait fulfilled the stated objective of the U.N. economic sanctions. Nevertheless, the United States government insisted upon continuing the stringent economic sanctions upon Iraq. The intent was to force the people of Iraq to remove Saddam from power, even though it is illegal under international law to punish a population in order to provoke it to overthrow the government. Unfortunately, the original U.N. resolution did not provide for automatic withdrawal of the sanctions upon Saddam's compliance with its requirements to remove his forces from Kuwait; rather, the resolution's language required the passage of a new Security Council resolution to relax or abolish the sanctions. According to Security Council rules, however, any of the five permanent members of the Security Council can veto any new resolution. Over the next 12 years the United States—sometimes joined by Great Britain—made clear its objection to any lifting of the sanctions and vetoed periodic attempts by other nations to end them. In other words, although these were technically United Nations sanctions, they continued *only* because of United States insistence.

> *The United Nations estimated that half a million Iraqi children died between 1991 and 1998 because of the [US-backed] sanctions, most from malnutrition and waterborne disease.*

Given the previous devastation of Iraqi infrastructure, however, the severity of these sanctions was so extreme that the catastrophic effect on the civilian population (including the deaths of countless civilians) was predictable and inevitable. Indeed, documents obtained later reveal that senior officials within the United States government were well aware of the impact that the sanctions would have upon civilians. Specifically banned by the sanctions, for instance, were replacement parts required to repair the damaged electrical power plants, sanitation infrastructure and water-purification facilities throughout the country. Millions of Iraqis would be drinking contaminated water. The United States maintained these highly lethal sanctions until after the beginning of the Iraq war in May 2003.

While the exact number of casualties is unknown, the United Nations estimated that half a million Iraqi children died between 1991 and 1998 because of the sanctions, most from malnutrition and waterborne disease. Before the 1991 war and the economic sanctions, Iraq had been one of the most advanced countries in the Middle East, with low childhood mortality, high levels of education and relative freedom for women. Although the 1995 U.N. Oil-for-Food Program allowed Iraq to sell some of its oil for food and certain medications, the sanctions remained brutal, preventing repair of the electrical grid or sanitation systems. As a result, hundreds of thousands of Iraqis, especially children, died; hundreds of thousands more were permanently affected by malnutrition and disease. . . .

Pervasive Militarism

I believe that my country has become something different— almost opposite to—the country most Americans believe we live in. We see ourselves as benign. We see ourselves as the light of the world. We interpret our actions—whether military adventures, economic initiatives or cultural exports—as good and as welcomed by the rest of the world. (In 2005, a majority of Americans believed that most people in the world supported the invasion of Iraq!) We see ourselves as the (perhaps somewhat tarnished) white knight. In other words, we are holding on to a vision that might have had some truth in it right after World War II but that no longer holds true. We see ourselves as a great hope for the rest of the world; others see us as "the greatest danger to world peace."

Although it now shocks me how long it has taken me, how much evidence I previously hid from, only recently have I become conscious of the pervasiveness of American militarism, how it defines who we are and how we are perceived. What do I mean by "militarism?" I mean a general belief within a country that an overpowering military is necessary for national security and a general willingness to spend virtually unlimited funds for that purpose. Militarism means a national conviction that the country must be prepared to use its military power aggressively to maintain its interests. In practical terms, it means that the nation is prepared to turn very quickly toward military solutions to international problems without allowing other measures a real chance to work. The threat of military response becomes ever-present in international conflict and so becomes, at least as far as other countries are concerned, our first response to conflict.

Consider a few examples over the last years: It is militarism that breaks off reasonably successful diplomatic negotiations with North Korea, labeling the country among the "axis of evil" and making take-it-or-leave-it demands not so subtly backed up by our military. It is militarism when the nation refuses to consider internationally coordinated police and intelligence action as a response to [terrorist group] al-Qaida's attack on 9/11, but instead insists on invading Afghanistan. It is militarism to refuse to allow the United Nations inspections team to finish its work in Iraq (no weapons of mass destruction had been found) in order to invade in 2003. It is militarism that rebuffs a direct high-level appeal to the Bush administration from Iran (in 2003) to enter into negotiations (in which Iran had suggested trading its nuclear aspirations for a guaranteed non-aggression pact), instead labeling Iran among the "axis of evil" and then leaking repeated threats to invade or bomb military targets.

Since 1941, the United States has been continuously engaged in, or mobilized for, war. That that fact does not seriously disturb or even surprise most of us is a powerful sign of how inured we have become to our nation's militarization. After conflicts prior to World War II, the United States disbanded or sharply reduced its combat forces and military budget when the fighting was over. But instead of reining in our military after World War II, we entered immediately into the Cold War. Even after the demise of the Soviet Union when there was literally no military threat, our military spending barely hiccuped as we continued our mobilization for war. In addition to the massive expenditures in the Cold War, between the end of World War II and 9/11, the United States conducted approximately 200 overseas military operations in which our forces attacked first. In no case did a democratic government come about as a direct result, although we installed and protected numerous dictators, including the Shah of Iran, Suharto in Indonesia, [Fulgencio] Batista in Cuba, [Anastasio] Somoza in Nicaragua, [Augusto] Pinochet in Chile and Mobutu [Sese Seko] in Congo/Zaire, not to mention the series of American-backed militarists in South Vietnam and Cambodia. For decades we also ran what can only be called terrorist operations against Cuba and, for a shorter time, in Nicaragua. . . .

We Americans have allowed our assumptions that we're the good guys—that we're acting in the best interests of justice, peace and democracy—to blind us to the reality of the death and destruction we are responsible for. Even several years after the American invasion of Iraq, when it had become clear that there had been no weapons of mass destruction and that Saddam Hussein had never been a threat to us, close, well-meaning friends kept assuring me that "President Bush knows something that he can't tell us." And now that it is clear that the president had no secret information, many are blaming him for the disaster. But Iraq is atypical only in that the thin-to-nonexistent rationale for invasion has been so clearly exposed. But Iraq is no different in kind from dozens of other military and covert actions that we have unilaterally and illegally taken in the last 50 years—from Vietnam to Nicaragua to Panama to Grenada. . . .

The United States military must become what most Americans believe it should be—a defensive force that protects the United States from attack.

Alternatives to Militarism

Unfortunately, there is almost complete agreement among American political leaders that we need more, rather than less, military power and military spending. Even President-elect Barack Obama is part of the post-World War II, bipartisan consensus that views unchallengeable military strength as essential. In his campaign, at least, he called for *increased* spending on the military. Although he has called for withdrawal from Iraq, he has also called for moving those troops to Afghanistan, a move that will be as futile as the Soviet attempt to tame Afghanistan in the 1980s, unless the endeavor becomes something very different from a *military* campaign.

What are the alternatives? First, and most importantly, the United States military must become what most Americans believe it should be—a defensive force that protects the United States from attack. The nearly 1,000 military bases around the world need to be dismantled, and its personnel brought home. Our country must strongly repudiate the pre-emptive-war doctrine of the 2002 National Security Strategy, give up our self-proclaimed role as the globe's police, and follow European nations' examples of having a purely defensive military.

Second, we must take the lead in world nuclear disarmament. After the fall of the Soviet Union, Russia and the other former Soviet states were eager for the abolishment of nuclear weapons, but the United States government refused to consider disarmament. Instead, we have refused to honor our commitments under the Nuclear Non-Proliferation Treaty, withdrawn from the Anti-Ballistic Missile Treaty and refused to enter into the Comprehensive Test Ban Treaty. The recent tensions between India and Pakistan (while highlighting the hesitation of nuclear powers to engage in open warfare), and the possibility that the political instability of Pakistan would leave nuclear weapons in the hands of Islamic fundamentalists underscore the necessity to abolish these weapons from the face of the Earth. Over the last 20 years, the militarism of the United States has been the greatest barrier to their abolition. We must take the lead in destroying them and leading other nations to do the same.

Third, we must strengthen capacity for international police action. For some time to come, international aimed force against terrorist and other dangerous groups will be necessary, but this force must be deployed as police action not as war. (Military attacks always kill and wound civilians and damage civilian infrastructure, leading inevitably to the creation of new antagonisms and through them to the recruiting of new terrorists.) The world's current ability to provide such police force has been hampered by the U.S. insistence on being the sole world policeman. Intelligence services and cooperation with other nations to arrest terrorists as "criminals" (rather than the "freedom fighters" they become in military conflict) is the model used by other Western nations and would be far more productive (and far less expensive) than our current military model. Our country needs to encourage the strengthening of the United Nations or other such international organization that could provide military force when needed in failed states or situations of gross human rights abuses.

Finally, we must use the hundreds of billions of dollars saved from disarmament to provide foreign aid to underdeveloped countries. The growth of terrorism and the failure of states stems directly from poverty and ignorance. Providing enough food, shelter, basic education and adequate health care for everyone in the world is, relatively speaking, not an expensive endeavor, certainly less than we've been spending in Iraq. Only the development of the Third World will give us the potential for freedom from terror. . . . As Kevin Phillips outlines in his book, *Wealth and Democracy*, a primary cause of the decline of the last three Western empires (Spain, Holland and Great Britain) has been bankruptcy through militarization.

As each of these empires became wealthy and powerful, it attempted to maintain its world position through military spending, each time imagining that its wealth and power were limitless. In each case, the vast military expenditures crippled the empire, leading directly to its decline. It should be obvious that the United States is well into this process of damaging itself with its own military expenditures. With a $10 trillion debt (much of it to countries that could easily use it against us) and an annual deficit that has been running close to $500 billion, the time is ripe to push for a maximum reduction in military spending (that could reduce the average deficit to zero). While our nation does not have moral right to forego those aspects of the military budget that pay for past wars (primarily veterans' benefits), transforming our military from an offensive weapon into an institution for national defense would be an affirmation of American principles stated in our founding documents, while saving our country from the historical course of all empires that turn toward militarism.

2

It Is the Political Left, Not the World, That Hates America

Dennis Prager

Dennis Prager is a radio show host, a contributing columnist for
Townhall.com, *and author of* Happiness is a Serious Problem:
A Human Nature Repair Manual.

Many people believe the world hates America. In fact, however,
much of the world loves America. Many people, for example,
want to emigrate to and live in America. It is only the left
around the world that dislikes America and its values. This is
because American religious certainty and willingness to use vio-
lence against evil is a threat to the values of the left throughout
the world. Similarly, the American left is committed to many
anti-American values and seems at times to embrace anti-
Americanism.

One of the most widely held beliefs in the contemporary world—so widely held it is not disputed—is that, with few exceptions, the world hates America. One of the Democrats' major accusations against the [George W.] Bush administration is that it has increased hatred of America to unprecedented levels. And in many polls, the United States is held to be among the greatest obstacles to world peace and harmony.

The World Left and the U.S.

But it is not true that the world hates America. It is the world's left that hates America. However, because the left dominates the world's news media and because most people, understandably, believe what the news media report, many people, including Americans, believe that the world hates America.

That it is the left—and those influenced by the left-leaning news and entertainment media—that hates America can be easily shown.

Take Western Europe, which is widely regarded as holding America in contempt, but upon examination only validates our thesis. The French, for example, are regarded as particularly America-hating, but if this were so, how does one explain the election of Nicolas Sarkozy as president of France? Sarkozy loves America and was known to love America when he ran for president. Evidently, it is the left in France—a left that, like the left in America, dominates the media, arts, universities and unions—that hates the U.S., not the French.

The same holds true for Spain, Australia, Britain, Latin America and elsewhere. The left in these countries hate the United States while non-leftists, and especially conservatives, in those countries hold America in high regard, if not actually love it.

Take Spain. The prime minister of Spain from 1996 to 2004, Jose Maria Aznar, is a conservative who holds America in the highest regard. He was elected twice, and polls in Spain up to the week before the 2004 election all predicted a third term for Aznar's party (Aznar had promised not to run for a third term). Only the Madrid subway bombings, perpetrated by Muslim terrorists three days before the elections, but which the Aznar government erroneously blamed on Basque separatists, turned the election against the conservative party.

People Want to Come to America

There is another obvious argument against the belief that the world hates America: Many millions of people would rather live in America than in any other country. How does the left explain this? Why would people want to come to a country they loathe? Why don't people want to live in Sweden or France as much as they wish to live in America? Those are rich and free countries, too.

The answer is that most people know there is no country in the world more accepting of strangers as is America. After three generations, people who have emigrated to Germany or France or Sweden do not feel—and are not regarded as—fully German, French or Swedish. Yet, anyone of any color from any country is regarded as American the moment he or she identifies as one. The country that the left routinely calls "xenophobic" and "racist" is in fact the least racist and xenophobic country in the world.

America, and especially the most hated parts of America—conservatives, religious conservatives in particular—are the greatest obstacles to leftist dominance.

Given that it is the left and the institutions it dominates—universities, media (other than talk radio in America) and unions—that hate America, two questions remain: Why does the left hate America, and does the American left, too, hate America?

The answer to the first question is that America and especially the most hated parts of America—conservatives, religious conservatives in particular—are the greatest obstacles to leftist dominance. American success refutes the socialist ideals of the left; American use of force to vanquish evil refutes the left's pacifist tendencies; America is the last great country that believes in putting some murderers to death, something that is anathema to the left; when America is governed by conservatives, it uses the language of good and evil, language regarded by the left as "Manichean"; most Americans still believe in the Judeo-Christian value system, another target of the left because the left regards all religions as equally valid (or more to the point, equally foolish and dangerous) and regards God-based morality as the moral equivalent of alchemy.

It makes perfect sense that the left around the world loathes America. The final question, then, is whether this loathing of America is characteristic of the American left as well. The answer is that the American left hates the America that believes in American exceptionalism, is prepared to use force to fight what it deems as dangerous evil, affirms the Judeo-Christian value system, believes in the death penalty, supports male-female marriage, rejects big government, wants lower taxes, prefers free market to governmental solutions, etc. The American left, like the rest of the world's left, loathes that America.

So what America does the American left love? That is for those on the left to answer. But given their beliefs that America was founded by racists and slaveholders, that it is an imperialist nation, that 35 million Americans go hungry, that it invades countries for corporate profits, and that it is largely racist and xenophobic, it is a fair question.

3

The Political Right Dishonors American Values

Mitchell Bard

Mitchell Bard is a writer and independent filmmaker.

Conservative leaders argue that the left hates America. However, America has always stood for freedom and democracy. By embracing torture and the dismissal of due process, conservatives have set themselves against America's most important values. Therefore, it is conservatives, not liberals, who oppose America and what it stands for.

On Sunday, as I sat watching former House speaker Newt Gingrich unabashedly endorse the politics of fear on *Meet the Press*, ("I think people should be afraid"), I couldn't help wonder why so many Republicans hate America so much.

American Values

Don't get me wrong. I know Republicans think they love America. They talk a lot about how much they love America. And they were quick to question the patriotism of anyone who opposed the [George W] Bush administration's policies after the 9/11 attacks. But do they?

Yes, I know, I'm being a wise guy to make a point. But when Gingrich talks, it seems like he opposes the basic principles of freedom and due process that for centuries have defined what it means to be an American.

Gingrich, after forecasting doom if Guantanamo [an American prison for terrorist suspects in Guantanamo Bay, Cuba] is closed down (Terrorists will recruit in our prisons!), even defended torture and Guantanamo by saying, "[W]hat's your highest priority? Is it to defend America and protect American lives, or is it to find some way to defend terrorists and to get terrorists involved in the criminal justice system?", adding that "only" three targets were tortured. (As [commentator] Keith Olbermann asked last night, is only committing three crimes, hundreds of times, a defense to those crimes?)

Gingrich defended the Bush policies in these words:

And so they did everything for seven and a half years to— and they have a very simple principle: If you're in doubt, do what it takes to help America survive every time. So they consistently fell down on the side of being very tough about national security, being very tough with specific terrorists.

He also explained his thought process:

The question is, is the most important thing to us today to find some kind of civil—American Civil Liberties Union model of making sure that we never offend terrorists, or is the model for us today to say to the CIA and others, 'Do everything you can to protect America. . . .'" But here's the thing: Gingrich talks about defending America, but he and his pro-Guantanamo, pro-torture crew are not defending America, at least as it has been identified by presidents from Franklin Roosevelt to Ronald Reagan to even George W. Bush. In fact, the America that we have defended from World War II through W.'s administration seems to be something Gingrich, Dick Cheney [vice-president under George W. Bush] and those that agree with them feel comfortable disposing of.

Freedom vs. Tyranny

Every U.S. conflict of the 20th century has been explained as some variation of freedom fighting tyranny. That quality, it was said, is what made America special. We had a free society, with a democratically elected government that followed the laws of the land. We bragged about the lack of succession challenges when Richard Nixon resigned noting that even though Gerald Ford had never been elected president or vice president by the American people, his legitimacy was never questioned, since his ascension to office followed the process set out in our laws.[1] World War II was a battle between democracy and fascism. The Cold War was about freedom versus Communist repression.

Iraq was to be a beacon of freedom, Bush liked to tell us. He said the terrorists hated us for our freedoms.

Even in the 21st century, Bush spoke a lot about freedom. One of the 1,876 justifications (I may be exaggerating a tad) offered by Bush for the Iraq war after no weapons of mass destruction were found was to provide Iraqis with democracy and freedom. Iraq was to be a beacon of freedom, Bush liked to tell us. He said the terrorists hated us for our freedoms.

But those freedoms seem irrelevant to Gingrich and Cheney, at least with regards to torture and Guantanamo.

Republicans deify Ronald Reagan for standing in West Berlin and saying, "Mr. Gorbachev, tear down this wall." But Reagan wasn't talking about lousy architecture. Rather, he was saying that on one side of the wall lived the good guys who enjoyed democratic freedoms, and on the other side resided people who had no freedom and lived under the oppression

---

1. Gerald Ford was appointed vice-president in 1973 following the resignation due to scandal of Spiro Agnew.

of the bad guys, the Communists. It was the guys in the East that did things, like, say, torturing people and holding them without charging them, while such atrocities would never go on in the West.

But what if the governments on both sides of the wall tortured people and held suspects without trial? What then? Would Reagan's words have meant anything?

What Are We Fighting For?

They've reduced defending America to rooting for a sport team, where you just want your club to win.

That is the very question facing Gingrich and Cheney now. If we torture and hold suspects without trial, where is our moral high ground? Can we torture and be Reagan's good guys? What are we fighting for? I thought the whole point of the war on terror is to defend the American way of life. But if we surrender our values to fight the war, to use a popular saw, haven't the terrorists won?

It seems to me that the Cheney/Gingrich crowd have no interest in protecting this America, the America of freedom and due process. Rather, they want to protect America as one side of a conflict, without regard to the very values that they purport to be fighting for. It's as if they've reduced defending America to rooting for a sports team, where you just want your club to win.

So when Gingrich says, "Do everything you can to protect America," or, "Is it to defend America and protect American lives, or is it to find some way to defend terrorists and to get terrorists involved in the criminal justice system?", he is missing the point completely. If we do everything we can to protect America, including discarding the freedom and due process that is at the heart of American values, what are we protecting? . . .

People like Gingrich and Cheney (and most of the Republicans in Congress) have a view of America that is completely out of sync with what America has meant over the last century, including what Reagan was drawing on when he made his speech in West Berlin. The America that Cheney and Gingrich see is one in which it's more about us versus them than preserving the very qualities that make America something worth defending.

That is why I say that Cheney and Gingrich don't love America. Because they don't seem to care about American values as they have traditionally been viewed. At least before Bush took over the White House.

4

Islam Does Not Hate America, But Objects to Its Policies

John L. Esposito

John L. Esposito is a professor of religion and international affairs and of Islamic studies at Georgetown University.

The Muslim religion is not especially focused on violence, and does not call for the destruction of all non-Muslims. "Jihad" refers primarily to self-struggle and striving for holiness, not to holy war. Terrorists claim that they are following Islam when they use violence, but this is a perversion of the Muslim tradition. The main impetus to Muslim violence are local political struggles, not religion. Similarly, the Islamic world resents the US not because of religion, but because of America's foreign policies, such as the invasion of Iraq and the support of Israel.

Jihad (exertion or struggle) is sometimes referred to as the Sixth Pillar of Islam. The importance of jihad is rooted in the Quran's command to struggle (the literal meaning of the word *jihad*) in the path of God and in the example of the Prophet Muhammad and his early Companions.

What Is Jihad?

The history of the Muslim community from Muhammad to the present can be read within the framework of what the Quran teaches about jihad. These Quranic teachings are significant to Muslim self-understanding, piety, mobilization, expansion, and defense. Jihad as struggle pertains to the difficulty and complexity of living a good life: struggling against the evil in oneself—to be virtuous and moral, making a serious effort to do good works and help to reform society. Depending on the circumstances in which one lives, it also can mean fighting injustice and oppression, spreading and defending Islam, and creating a just society through preaching, teaching, and, if necessary, armed struggle or holy war.

Jihad refers to the obligation incumbent on all Muslims, individuals and the community, to follow and realize God's will.

The two broad meanings of jihad, nonviolent and violent, are contrasted in a well-known Prophetic tradition. It is said that when Muhammad returned from battle he told his followers, "We return from lesser jihad [warfare] to the greater jihad." The greater jihad is the more difficult and more important struggle against one's ego, selfishness, greed, and evil.

In its most general meaning, jihad refers to the obligation incumbent on all Muslims, individuals and the community, to follow and realize God's will: to lead a virtuous life and to extend the Islamic community through preaching, education, example, writing, etc. Jihad also includes the right, indeed the obligation, to defend Islam and the community from aggression. Throughout history, the call to jihad has rallied Muslims to the defense of Islam. An example of this is the Afghan *mujahidin* [resistance fighters] who fought a decade-long jihad (1979–89) against Soviet occupation.

Jihad is a concept with multiple meanings, used and abused throughout Islamic history. Although it is not associated with the words *holy war* anywhere in the Quran, Muslim rulers, with the support of religious scholars and officials, have historically used the concept of armed jihad to legitimate wars of imperial expansion. Early extremist groups also appealed to Islam to legitimate rebellion, assassination, and attempts to overthrow Muslim rulers.

In recent years religious extremists and terrorists have insisted that jihad is a universal religious obligation and that all true Muslims must join the jihad to promote a global Islamic revolution. A radicalized minority have combined militancy with messianic visions to mobilize an "army of God" whose jihad is to "liberate" Muslims at home and abroad. They have engaged in acts of violence and terror in their attempts to topple Muslim governments and, like Osama bin Laden [the leader of al Qaeda, the group responsible for the 9/11 terrorist attacks.] and others, engaged in a global jihad.

Is There a Global Jihad Today?

Although jihad has been throughout the centuries and still is an important belief and practice, since the last half of the twentieth century, a globalization of jihad has occurred in religious thought and in action. On the one hand, jihad's primary Quranic religious and spiritual aspects—the "struggle" or effort to follow God's path, to lead a good life—remain central to Muslim spirituality. On the other hand, the concept of armed jihad has became more widespread, and has been used by resistance and liberation movements, as well as by extremist and terrorist organizations to legitimate, recruit, and motivate their followers.

From the late 1970s to the early 1990s, Muslim extremist groups primarily focused their attention locally, within their own countries. With the exception of bombings at the World Trade Center in 1993 and in Paris in 1995, most attacks against Westerners occurred within Muslim countries, from Morocco, Egypt, Saudi Arabia, and Turkey to Iraq, Yemen, Pakistan, and Indonesia. America and Europe remained secondary targets, "the far enemy." But because of their military and economic support for oppressive regimes, hatred and fear of Western nations continued to build.

The 1979–89 Soviet-Afghan war marked a turning point; jihad went global in an unprecedented way. The globalization of the war in Afghanistan could be seen in the countries that supported it, the mass communications that covered it, and the way in which the mass media made it an immediate reality around the world. It took place during the Cold War, at a time when Western and many Muslim nations feared both the spread of Communism and [the Ayatollah] Khomeini's export of the Iranian revolution. While many in America, Europe, Pakistan, Saudi Arabia, and the Gulf States condemned Iran's "evil" jihad, both Western and Muslim governments embraced and were anxious to support Afghanistan's "good" jihad against the Soviets with money, weapons, and advisers. The globalization of communications, technology, and travel heightened a new consciousness of the transnational identity and interconnectedness of the Islamic community (*ummah*). Events in Afghanistan were followed across the Muslim world on a daily, hourly basis. This reinforced a sense of solidarity and identification with this righteous struggle. The *mujahidin* holy war drew Muslims from many parts of the world. Regardless of their national origin, these fighters came to be called the Afghan Arabs.

Terrorists like bin Laden and others go beyond classical Islam's criteria for a just jihad and recognize no limits but their own, employing any weapons and any means.

In the aftermath of the Afghan war, the new global jihad became the common symbol and rallying cry for holy and unholy wars. The mujahidin and Taliban in Afghanistan and Muslims in Bosnia, Chechnya, Kashmir, Kosovo, the southern Philippines, and Uzbekistan cast their armed struggles as jihads. Hizbollah, [in Lebanon] Hamas (the Islamic Resistance Movement), [in the Gaza strip] and Islamic Jihad Palestine have characterized violence and opposition against Israel as jihad. Al-Qaeda (the Base), through leader Osama bin Laden, claimed to be waging a global jihad against corrupt Muslim governments and the West.

Afghan Arabs moved on to fight other jihads in their home countries and in Bosnia, Kosovo, and Central Asia. Others stayed on or were trained and recruited in the new jihadi madrasas [religious schools] and training camps.

An outgrowth of the Afghan war was the development of a global jihad ideology among militants who saw Afghanistan as but one step in a global war against "un-Islamic" Muslim governments and the West. The policies of many authoritarian and oppressive Muslim regimes proved to be catalysts for radicalization and terrorism both within their countries and directed toward their Western supporters.

Al-Qaeda (modern in its use of technology: computers, faxes, Internet, cell phones, weapons), its affiliates, and other radical groups represent a new form of terrorism, born of transnationalism and globalization. They are transnational in identity and recruitment and global in ideology, strategy, targets, network of organizations, and economic transactions. Individuals and groups, religious and lay, have seized the right to declare and legitimate unholy wars in the name of Islam.

Terrorists like bin Laden and others go beyond classical Islam's criteria for a just jihad and recognize no limits but their own, employing any weapons and any means. They reject Islamic law's regulations regarding the goals and means of a valid jihad; that violence must be proportional and that only the necessary amount of force should be used to repel the enemy; that innocent civilians should not be targeted; and that jihad must be declared by the ruler or head of state.

Is Islam a Primary Cause and Driver of Terrorism?

Islam, like every other world religion, neither supports nor requires illegitimate violence. The Quran does not advocate or condone terrorism. To enhance their credibility and justify their atrocities, terrorists connect their acts of violence to Islam by ignoring the extensive limits that the Quran and the Islamic tradition place on the use of violence. As happens in other faiths, a radical fringe distorts and misinterprets mainstream and normative Islamic doctrines and laws. They pay no attention to Islamic law, which draws on the Quran to set out clear guidelines for the conduct of war and provides no support for hijacking and hostage taking.

Throughout the Quran, Muslims are urged to be merciful and just. However, Islam does give guidelines to Muslims for defending their families and themselves as well as their religion and community from aggression. The earliest Quranic verses dealing with the right to engage in a "defensive" struggle, were revealed shortly after Muhammad and his followers escaped persecution in Mecca by emigrating to Medina. At a time when they were forced to fight for their lives, Muhammad was told: "Leave is given to those who fight because they were wronged—surely God is able to help them— who were expelled from their homes wrongfully for saying, 'Our Lord is God'" (22:39–40).

Throughout the Quran, Muslims are urged to be merciful and just.

Like the Hebrew scriptures or Old Testament, the Quran contains verses about struggles and wars. The Islamic community developed in Arabia, in the city of Mecca, where Muhammad lived and received God's revelation. The city was assailed by cycles of tribal warfare and surrounded by constant conflicts between the Byzantine (Eastern Roman) and the Sasanian (Persian) empires. Nevertheless, the Quranic verses repeatedly stress that peace must be the norm. The Quran frequently and strongly balances permission to fight in enemy by mandating the need to make peace: "If your enemy inclines toward peace, then you too should seek peace and put your trust in God" (8:61).

Those concerned about Islam and violence often point to what some refer to as the "sword verse" (although the word *sword* does not appear in the Quran). This oft-cited verse is seen as encouraging Muslims to kill unbelievers: "When the sacred months have passed, slay the idolaters wherever you find them, and take them, and confine them, and lie in wait for them at every place of ambush" (9:5). Critics use the verse to demonstrate that Islam is inherently violent, while religious extremists twist its meaning to develop a theology of hate and intolerance and to justify unconditional warfare against unbe-lievers. In fact, it is a distortion to apply this passage to all non-Muslims or unbelievers; the verse is specifically referring to Meccan "idolaters" who are accused of breaking a treaty and continuously warring against the Muslims. Moreover, crit-ics do not mention that this "sword verse" is immediately qualified by the following: "But if they repent and fulfill their devotional obligations and pay the zakat [the charitable tax on non-Muslims], then let them go their way, for God is forgiv-ing and kind" (9:5).

Religion and Nationalism

The religious language and symbolism used by extremists ob-scures Islam's true relationship to violence and terrorism, as well as the primary causes of global terrorism. It becomes easy for policymakers and experts to point to religion as the root cause of terrorism and violence. In most cases, complex politi-cal and economic grievances are the primary catalysts for con-flicts, but religion becomes a means to legitimate the cause and mobilize popular support. As we can see in the global strategy of Osama bin Laden and al-Qaeda or witness in Pal-estine, post-Saddam [Hussein] Iraq, or Kashmir, the goals of terrorists are often basically nationalist: to end the occupation of lands, to force "foreign" military forces out of what they see as their homeland.

Of course religion does provide a powerful source of meaning and motivation. Its invocation lends divine authority that increases a terrorist leader's own authority as well as moral justification, obligation, certitude, and heavenly reward, all of which enhance recruitment and produce the willingness to fight and die in a "sacred struggle." Secular movements have also hijacked religion to heighten their appeal. Yasser Arafat, leader of a secular nationalist movement in Palestine (PLO [Palestine Liberation Organization] and then PNA [Palestinian National Authority]), drew on the power of religious symbolism when he was under siege in Ramallah by using the terms *jihad* and *shahid* (martyr) to describe his situation. The Palestinian militia (not just the Islamist Hamas) chose to call itself the al-Aqsa Martyrs Brigade, using the symbolism of the al-Aqsa Mosque (the holy site for Islam and Judaism in Jerusalem) and drawing on the imagery of jihad and martyrdom. While religious and nonreligious organizations and movements (whether al-Qaeda or the Marxist Tamil Tigers in Sri Lanka) may share common strategy, those that are Muslim often strengthen their cause by identifying their goal as Islamic: to create an Islamic government, a caliphate, or simply a more Islamically oriented state and society.

Religious leaders and intellectuals can play an important role in the ideological war on terror. Wahhabi Islam and militant Christian Right groups do not advocate violence or error. However, both promote exclusivist, nonpluralistic theologies of hate that condemn other faiths and can be used by militants. Hate speech is a powerful justification for blowing up the Twin Towers of the World Trade Center, government buildings or abortion clinics—for assassinating "the enemies of God." Christians and Muslims share a critical common goal, that of addressing exclusivist theologies that are antipluralistic and weak on tolerance. For these theologies contribute to beliefs, attitudes, and values that feed religious extremism and terrorism that affects all of us. . . .

Muslim rulers and governments past and present have used religion to legitimate and mobilize support for political expansion and imperialism.

Why Are Muslims So Violent?

The acts of Muslim extremists in recent years lead many to ask why Islam and Muslims are so violent. Islam, from the Quran to Islamic law, does not permit terrorism and places limits on the use of violence. It does permit, and in some circumstances even requires, the use of force in self-defense or the defense of Islam and the Islamic community. However, there is often a fine line between legitimate and illegitimate use of force, defensive and offensive battle and warfare, resistance and terrorism. While religion can be a powerful force for good, historically it has also been used to legitimate violence and warfare. The three great monotheistic traditions from biblical times to the present represent long histories of the positive and negative power of religion, its ability to create and to destroy.

Muslim rulers and governments past and present have used religion to legitimate and mobilize support for political expansion and imperialism. Religious extremists from early groups such as the Kharijites to contemporary movements like Egypt's Islamic Jihad and al-Qaeda have employed a radical theological vision, based upon distorted interpretations of scripture and doctrine, to justify violence and terrorism against their own societies and the international community. They have created a world in which those who do not accept and follow their beliefs, Muslim and non-Muslim alike, are the enemy to be fought and exterminated by any means.

The violent character of many states compounds the issue of violence in Muslim societies further. Authoritarian rulers and governments, secular and religious, use force, violence, repression, and terror to assure their stability and security at home and, in some instances, to expand their influence abroad. Failed economies, high unemployment, shortages of housing, a growing gap between rich and poor, and widespread corruption exacerbate the situation, contributing to the growth of radicalism and extremist opposition. The extent to which outside powers, including America and Europe, are seen as supporting oppressive regimes or "colonizing" and exploiting Muslim societies contributes to the appeal of violence and terrorism. These conditions and grievances create a seedbed from which the Saddam Husseins and Osama bin Ladens of the world find ready recruits in their unholy wars. . . .

Why Do They Hate Us?

Anti-Americanism (along with anti-Europeanism) is a broad-based phenomenon that cuts across Arab and Muslim societies. It is driven not only by the blind hatred or religious zealotry of extremists but also by frustration and anger with U.S. foreign policy among a mainstream majority in the Muslim world.

Terrorists want to kill us, but most Muslims want us to stop making the world an even more dangerous place.

While many continue to believe anti-Americanism is tied to insurmountable religious and cultural differences, the facts undercut this simple and rather self-serving response.

Terrorists may hate America (and some European countries), but the rest of the Muslim world does not. We fail to distinguish between the hatred of extremists and a broad anti-Americanism among those who admire our accomplishments, principles, and values but denounce what they see as

U.S. arrogance, unilateralism, and hegemonic designs. Terrorists want to kill us, but most Muslims want us to stop making the world an even more dangerous place.

Major polls (Gallup, PEW, Zogby, and others) of the beliefs and attitudes of a cross-section of Muslims around the world give us a good measure of their admiration as well as their resentment, which, left unaddressed, has the potential to increase radicalization.

Gallup World Polls from 2001 to 2009 in more than thirty-five Muslim countries from North Africa to Southeast Asia, representing the voices of a billion Muslims, have shown the importance of policy as the primary driver or catalyst.

Sixty-six percent of Kuwaitis have unfavorable views of the United States, but only 3 percent see Canada unfavorably.

Muslims do not see all Western countries as the same. They distinguish between America and Europe and between specific European nations depending on their policies, not their culture or religion. During the pivotal years in the deterioration of U.S.-Muslim relations, Muslims globally drew a sharp distinction between America and Britain, under the [George W.] Bush and [Tony] Blair administrations, on the one hand, and other European countries, on the other. The United States and the United Kingdom were viewed negatively, while views of France and Germany were neutral to positive. For example, while 74 percent of Egyptians had unfavorable views of the United States, and 69 percent said the same about Britain, only 21 percent had unfavorable views of France and 29 percent of Germany. Across all predominantly Muslim countries polled, an average of 75 percent of respondents associate the word *ruthless* with the United States (in contrast to only 13 percent for France and 13 percent for Germany).

The importance of foreign policy emerges starkly when we compare Muslim views of the United States with views of Canada (America without its foreign policy, one might say). Sixty-six percent of Kuwaitis have unfavorable views of the United States, but only 3 percent see Canada unfavorably. Similarly, 64 percent of Malaysians say the United States is "aggressive"; yet only one in ten associates this quality with France and Germany.

Reactions to the U.S./U.K.-led invasion of Iraq underscore the influence of foreign policy on Muslim attitudes toward the West. When people in ten predominantly Muslim countries were asked how they view a number of nations, the attributes they most associate with the United States are "scientifically and technologically advanced" (68 percent), "aggressive" (66 percent), "conceited" (65 percent), and "morally decadent" (64 percent). Majorities in most countries who were asked about the invasion of Iraq, Muslim men and women alike, believed the invasion has done a great deal more harm than good. Muslims clearly have not seen their conflict as with the West or Western civilization as a whole but rather with specific Western powers' foreign policies.

The West's espousal of self-determination, democratization, and human rights is often seen as a hypocritical "double standard" when compared to its policies, what it actually does—for instance, supporting authoritarian Muslim regimes or imposing sanctions against Pakistan for its development of a nuclear weapon while failing to press Israel and India on their nuclear development. The moral will so evident in America's helping Kosovo is seen by many Muslims as totally absent in the U.S. policy of permissive neglect in the Chechnyan and Kashmiri conflicts. On the other hand, America's stance on human rights has been undermined by the abuse of Muslim prisoners in Abu Ghraib prison in Iraq and at Guantanamo Bay.

Globalization of communications has created a situation in which Arabs (Muslims and Christians) and Muslims around the world often see more than we see. Unlike the past, today international Arab and Muslim media are no longer solely dependent on Western reporters and channels. While America's overseas media presence (reporters and overseas posts) and coverage have waned over the past decade, television stations like Al-Jazeera, Al-Arabiyya, and others provide daily coverage of violence in many Muslim countries. They show, for example, the violence and acts of terror committed by both sides as well as the disproportionate firepower used against Palestinians by Israelis, America's record of overwhelming support for Israel—witnessed over the years in its levels of aid to Israel, the U.S. voting record in the United Nations, and official statements by the administration and State Department—has proved to be a powerful lightning rod for Muslim anger over injustice.

5

The Arab World Hates the US Because President Obama Is Weak

Michael Prell

Michael Prell is a former advisor to Israeli Prime Minister Benjamin Netanyahu and author of Underdogma: How America's Enemies Use our Love for the Underdog to Trash American Power.

President Barack Obama hoped that by apologizing for American power the Arab world would hate the United States less. Instead, a poll shows that the United States is less popular than ever in Arab nations. This is because the Arab world hates weakness. Obama has shown that the United States is weak, causing the Arab and Muslim world to despise America.

A new Zogby poll, "Arab Attitudes, 2011," has revealed that President Obama's charm offensive in the Arab world has failed. After he promised to restore America's international reputation, not only does the Arab world hate America more under Mr. Obama than it did under President George W. Bush, it even hates Mr. Obama—personally—more than it detested the swaggering unilateralist cowboy from Texas.

This news likely comes as a shock to Mr. Obama and his advisers, who thought that traveling the Arab world on a so-called "apology tour" and bowing down and bad-mouthing

American power would make the Arab world love America more—or at least make the Arabs love Mr. Obama more than Mr. Bush.

When Mr. Obama shows weakness and bows down and apologizes for American power, the Arab world sees him—and us—as a "weak horse."

But the numbers are in. Across the Arab world, Mr. Obama's favorability ratings are 10 percent or lower. That means the Arabs hate him more while he bows down to them than they hated Mr. Bush while he was bombing them.

Why is that?

Because the Arab world has a fundamentally different view of power.

The "Strong Horse" View of Power

There is an Arab proverb that says: "When people see a strong horse and a weak horse, by nature they will like the strong horse." This "strong horse" view of power is dominant in the Islamist world.

When Mr. Obama shows weakness and bows down and apologizes for American power, the Arab world sees him—and us—as a "weak horse." That doesn't make the Arabs love us more. It makes them hate us more because weakness is an affront to their strong-horse view of power.

But there is another consequence to Mr. Obama's weak-horse diplomacy.

Another Arab proverb says, "A falling camel attracts many knives." Weakness makes the Arabs want to stab the falling camel. That means that bowing down and apologizing for America's power does not make the Arabs love us more—it makes them want to kill us more. In their eyes, weakness is a signal, a justification—even a provocation—for violent attack.

How do we know this? They tell us and show us with their words and actions.

When al Qaeda attacked the USS Cole in October 2000 without any American reprisal, the terrorists could smell a weak horse. Their perception of American weakness, in their own words, inspired the architects of Sept. 11 to "end the legend of the so-called superpower that is America" by moving forward with murderous plans. The rest is history.

What effect is Mr. Obama's weak-horse diplomacy having in the Middle East? Let's consider what has changed in the Middle East in the two short years since the apologist in chief assumed office.

Recent Developments in the Middle East

In the Palestinian territories, where the people have rarely found a more vocal champion than in the Obama White House, 82 percent of Palestinians have an unfavorable view of the United States and they have felt emboldened to form an official coalition with the strong-horse internationally recognized terrorist group Hamas.

In Egypt, America's approval ratings have dropped since Mr. Obama's now-famous Cairo [in 2009] speech from 30 percent to 5 percent, and people are embracing the strong-horse Muslim Brotherhood as their next leader.

The Arab world never loved us, but at least it respected and feared American power.

Mr. Obama is the president who lost Turkey. In the short time that has passed since he bad-mouthed American history and power in his speech to the Turkish parliament, Turkey's approval rating for America has dropped to 14 percent. The once-secular Turkish nation has become more radicalized and Islamist, and Turkey has gone from being the vacation destination for Israeli tourists to one of Israel's biggest threats.

Since Mr. Obama showed the Arab world that he is a weak horse, Lebanon has been swallowed by [Islamic radical group] Hezbollah, Yemen is in chaos and is being taken over by al Qaeda, Pakistan gave refuge to Osama bin Laden [the Leader of al Qaeda] and then rounded up those who ratted him out. In Libya, where Mr. Obama waited five months to say [dictator] Moammar Gadhafi must go, the once-strong horse of America has shown the entire Arab world that it cannot dislodge one madman whom the whole world wants removed.

Just this week, Iran's President Mahmoud Ahmadinejad said in an unveiled threat to Israel and the broader world, "We have a saying in our language: 'If someone throws a smaller stone, you should respond with a bigger stone.' We will defend ourselves within our capabilities." That stands in stark contrast to Mr. Obama, who just last year announced to the world that America would not respond with its biggest stone—nuclear weapons—if it is attacked with a smaller stone.

The Arab world never loved us, but at least it respected and feared American power. Today, under Mr. Obama, the numbers show that a weak-horse America is less respected by the Arab world than a strong-horse America. Events in the Middle East show that the Arab world no longer respects or fears American power.

6

The Arab World Hates the US Because of President Obama's Militarism

Glenn Greenwald

Glenn Greenwald is a constitutional lawyer and writer. He blogs for Salon *and is the author of* With Liberty and Justice for Some: How the Law is Used to Destroy Equality and Protect the Powerful.

Polls show that Arab opinion of the United States has fallen even lower under the administration of President Barack Obama than it had during the George W. Bush administration. This is because the US has increased its use of violence in the region and continues to back dictatorial regimes and the oppressive policies of Israel. The US support for Libyan rebels who have committed numerous atrocities is one example of American hypocrisy and use of violence in the region.

I've written numerous times over the last year about rapidly worsening perceptions of the U.S. in the Muslim world, including a Pew poll from April finding that Egyptians view the U.S. more unfavorably now than they did during the Bush presidency. A new poll [conducted by IBOPE Zogby International] released today of six Arab nations—Egypt, Lebanon, Jordan, Saudi Arabia, the United Arab Emirates and Morocco—contains even worse news on this front:

Glenn Greenwald, "US More Unpopular in the Arab World Than Under Bush," Salon .com, July 13, 2011. © 2011 by Salon. This article first appeared in Salon.com, at http:// www.salon.com. An online version remains in the Salon archives. Reprinted with permission.

The hope that the Arab world had not long ago put in the United States and President [Barack] Obama has all but evaporated.

Two and a half years after Obama came to office, raising expectations for change among many in the Arab world, favorable ratings of the United States have plummeted in the Middle East, according to a new poll conducted by Zogby International for the Arab American Institute Foundation.

> In most countries surveyed, favorable attitudes toward the United States dropped to levels lower than they were during the last year of the Bush administration ... Pollsters began their work shortly after a major speech Obama gave on the Middle East ... Fewer than 10 percent of respondents described themselves as having a favorable view of Obama.

Escalating Violence

What's striking is that none of these is among the growing list of countries we're occupying and bombing. Indeed, several are considered among the more moderate and U.S.-friendly nations in that region, at least relatively speaking. Yet even in this group of nations, anti-U.S. sentiment is at dangerously (even unprecedentedly) high levels.

The very policies justified in the name of combating Terrorism are the same ones that do the most to sustain and perpetuate it.

In one sense, this is hardly surprising, given the escalating violence and bombing the U.S. is bringing to that region, its ongoing fealty to Israel, and the dead-ender support the American government gave to that region's besieged dictators. Though unsurprising, it's still remarkable. After all, one of the central promises of an Obama presidency was a re-making of America in the eyes of that part of the world, but the opposite is taking place.

More significantly, as democracy slowly but inexorably takes hold, consider the type of leaders that will be elected in light of this pervasive anti-American hostility. When the U.S. propped up dictators to suppress those populations, public opinion was irrelevant; now that that scheme is collapsing, public opinion will become far more consequential, and it does not bode well either for U.S. interests (as defined by the American government) or the U.S.'s ability to extract itself from its posture of Endless War in that region. Given that it is anti-American sentiment that, more than anything else, fuels Terrorism (as the Pentagon itself has long acknowledged), we yet again find the obvious truth: the very policies justified in the name of combating-Terrorism are the same ones that do the most to sustain and perpetuate it. . . .

While Americans are continuously inculcated with the message that Iran is the greatest threat to that region, the people who actually live there view the U.S. in that light.

The Greatest Threat to the Region

The full report on the new Middle East poll highlights several other additional striking findings:

> In five out of the six countries surveyed, *the U.S. was viewed less favorably than Turkey, China, France—or Iran.* Far from seeing the U.S. as a leader in the post-Arab Spring environment, the countries surveyed viewed *"U.S. interference in the Arab world" as the greatest obstacle to peace and stability* in the Middle East, second only to the continued Palestinian occupation. . . . President Obama's favorable ratings across the Arab world are *10% or less.*

While Americans are continuously inculcated with the message that Iran is the greatest threat to that region, the people who actually live there view the U.S. in that light. And

... that is a routine finding in surveys of Arab and Muslim opinion in that part of the world.

On a related note (related because the poll finds that "the U.S. role in establishing a no-fly zone over Libya[1] receives a positive rating only in Saudi Arabia and Lebanon, but, as an issue, it is the lowest priority"), this new *New York Times* article—detailing the atrocities committed by the Libyan rebels whom NATO is fighting to empower—is extraordinary for two reasons. First, that we're fighting to empower such barbaric factions obviously severely undercuts the humanitarian justifications offered for the war; as John Cole asks: "when do we start bombing to stop these war crimes?"

Second, as FAIR's [Fairness and Accuracy in Reporting] Jim Naureckas pointed out, the "NYT [*New York Times*] says rebel abuses 'paled next to' Gadhafi's—*then details virtually identical war crimes.*" To see how true that is, just marvel at these paragraphs, appearing one right after the next with no apparent editorial recognition of how contradictory they are:

> Colonel Qaddafi's soldiers have also been beaten at the point of capture, *and some have been shot,* including several prisoners in the besieged city of Misurata who were shot through the feet, either as a punishment or as a means to prevent escape.

> Rebels have also been seen by journalists repeatedly *firing makeshift rocket launchers indiscriminately into territory or towns held by the Qaddafi forces.*

> Such rebels actions, however, have paled next to the abuses of Colonel Qaddafi's forces, which have *fired on unarmed demonstrators and used artillery, rocket batteries and mortars against many rebel-held cities and towns.*

---

1. In 2011 the U.S. intervened in a Libyan Civil war to help topple Libyan dictator Muammar Qaddafi. Qaddafi was killed in October and a new government was formed.

The only thing more reliable than deaths and taxes is that the *NYT* will take the side of the U.S. Government in how it "reports" on any foreign conflict. And is there anything more predictable than the fact that the faction backed by the U.S. in a civil war turns out to be guilty of many of the same atrocities that "justified" the commencement of the war in the first place? Bask in the glow of humanitarianism.

7

European Love of President Obama Will Give Way to Anti-Americanism

Soeren Kern

Soeren Kern is Senior Fellow for Transatlantic Relations at the Madrid-based Strategic Studies Group.

The European press hated President George W. Bush. They were much more enthusiastic about his successor, Barack Obama. However, not long after Obama's election, the European press began to express disappointment and to move back toward anti-Americanism. The Europeans criticized Obama for continuing Bush's policies of military trials for Bush-era policies and for snubbing European heads of state. This shows that as long as America is the leading world power, it will provoke resentment, envy, and anti-Americanism in Europe.

On the campaign trail [in 2008], Barack Obama promised that he would "reboot America's image" around the world. Indeed, many Americans who voted for Obama believed that his global popularity would somehow reverse the tide of anti-Americanism that so vexed his predecessor. Echoing this sentiment of Obama as saviour of America's image abroad, presidential advisor David Axelrod recently asserted that "anti-Americanism isn't cool anymore."

A Return to Negativity

In Europe, where anti-Americanism was elevated to the status of a religion during the presidency of George W Bush, the "chattering classes" have, by and large, toned down their criticism of the United States since Obama was elected. In general, European media coverage of Obama has been quite favourable and the vehemence of the anti-American rhetoric has been notably more muted than in recent years. But now, five months into the age of Obama, the highly vaunted transatlantic honeymoon may be coming to an end. During the past several weeks, European media have started publishing stories that criticize Obama and once again cast the United States in a negative light. Could this be a harbinger of things to come?

But now, five months into the age of Obama, the highly vaunted transatlantic honeymoon may be coming to an end.

What follows is a brief selection of European news stories that typify what seems to be a general trend toward a return to more negative reporting about America, its people and its president.

In Britain, the left-leaning daily newspaper *The Independent* asks: "Has Obama been exposed as an innocent abroad?" It continues: "Barack Obama's foreign policy honeymoon may be petering out as events around the globe, whether in Israel, Iran or North Korea, conspire to expose some inconvenient realities about his vaunted olive-branch approach to international relations. A nicer America does not a nicer world immediately make. It would help if the 'Obama Effect' could be demonstrated actually to exist, even just a little."

In Germany, the news media have been especially angry over Obama's failure to close the prison for terrorist suspects at Guantánamo Bay in Cuba. The *Financial Times Deutschland*, in commentary titled "World's Hopes Dashed By George W. Obama," writes: "This decision [to revive military trials for some Guantánamo Bay detainees] isn't a belated insight, but the pathetic faltering of a man forced to confront a disastrous legacy.... No one who defends these institutions ought to criticise Islam's Sharia courts." The Munich-based center-left *Süddeutsche Zeitung*, in an editorial titled "Obama's Great Mistake," writes: "Obama's people certainly imagined things differently. But reality has caught up with them.... Bush light, so to speak... Obama is discrediting both himself and the United States."

Whenever [Obama] takes a step forward, he stumbles backwards as well.

German Newspapers

German newspapers have also been fiercely critical of Obama's refusal to release more photos of alleged torture at the Abu Ghraib prison in Iraq. The Berlin-based left-leaning daily *Die Tageszeitung* writes: "With his decision to prevent the publication of the photos, Obama, who promised transparency... is practicing opacity.... That the president is abdicating leadership on this question is a tragedy." In another commentary, *Die Tageszeitung* writes: "Whenever [Obama] takes a step forward, he stumbles backwards as well. That will likely be enough to disappoint all those Europeans who had expectations that Obama would be an almost messiah-like healer. It was expected that he would demolish all of the ugly monuments from the Bush era and then, together with Al Gore, plant a Garden of Eden over the top, through which he would drive fuel-efficient compacts from Chrysler."

The *Financial Times Deutschland* writes: "Obama promised that, under his leadership, politics in the US would be both more ethical and more transparent than ever before. The dark chapters of the Bush era would be illuminated as quickly as possible. But since Obama assumed a position of responsibility, it has become increasingly obvious that he cannot live up to these promises."

The Hamburg-based left-leaning *Der Spiegel*, which was one of the most hyperactive purveyors of anti-Americanism during the Bush presidency, has lately been back in full form. In recent weeks, the magazine has published a series of articles that are unusually critical of Obama. Some titles include: "From Mania to Distrust: Europe's Obama Euphoria Wanes," "Torturing for America," "American Gays and Lesbians Feel Betrayed by Obama," and "GM Insolvency Proves America's Global Power is Waning." . . .

Another *Der Spiegel* article is a quintessential example of the magazine's signature anti-American style. Titled "American Recession Food: The Fat Crisis," the article reports that millions of unemployed Americans are trying to save money by eating junk food at McDonalds. "The recession is leading to unemployment, waves of bankruptcies and the decline of entire neighbourhoods—and health and fitness problems for American citizens. Initial studies show that the crisis is impoverishing more and more people, which leads them to the most unhealthy and fatty foods. And this in an already obese and diabetic country." The article fails to mention, of course, that Europe in general, and Germany in particular, is facing its own obesity epidemic.

Eventually Europe Will Hate Obama

In Britain, the media have been parroting the same theme of America as a terminal wasteland. The center-right *Daily Telegraph* reports that "dozens of US cities may have entire neighbourhoods bulldozed as part of drastic 'shrink to survive' proposals being considered by the Obama administration to tackle economic decline. The left-wing *Guardian* warns that "far-right shootings raise fear of hate offensive in America." The killing of a black security guard at the Holocaust Museum in

Washington, DC is "the latest example of a surge in extremist violence, as the election of Barack Obama and the economic crisis breed resentment in a fanatical, racist minority," the *Guardian* asserts.

Many newspapers have expressed resentment over Obama's unwillingness to allow his European colleagues to bask in the limelight of joint photo opportunities.

In Switzerland, the St Gallen-based *Nachrichten.ch* asks whether America will go the way of General Motors. In a commentary, the paper writes: "The triumph of US ideology after the Second World War was in no small measure due to the positive associations connected to America. 'Brand USA' was attractive and appealing. But this attraction—just like the status of Cadillac as a dream car—is long since gone. Instead there is a general unease toward the United States, a country regarded as aggressive, financially ailing, the birthplace of a global recession and partly autistic when it comes to understanding the sensitivities of other countries and their cultures."

Underscoring the hypocrisy that underpins so much of the anti-Americanism in Europe, many newspapers have expressed resentment over Obama's unwillingness to allow his European colleagues to bask in the limelight of joint photo opportunities. Commenting on Obama's recent trip to Europe, the Brussels-based *EU Observer* ran a headline titled "Obama Keeps Leaders at Arm's Length on Europe Trip." It reported that Obama, much to the dismay of his French hosts, turned down a dinner invitation with French President Nicolas Sarkozy on top of the Eiffel tower.

Der Spiegel ran an article titled "Obama and Merkel: Trans-Atlantic Frenemies," which reports that the White House denied a request by German Chancellor Angela Merkel for face time with Obama. The magazine laments that "Germany is increasingly being left out of the loop." In an editorial, the *Neue Osnabrücker Zeitung* writes: "The radiance of German-American relations today has its limits. In the G-8, as in NATO and in Afghanistan, but also in Obama's itinerary, the waning importance of Germany is obvious." In another article, *Der Spiegel* quotes Sarkozy as mocking Merkel: "She can't even host the US president in the capital city," he bragged, while "I can meet him in Normandy and in Paris."

In Italy, the Turin-based *La Stampa* grieves for the future of Europe. It argues that Europe's political class is secretly resentful for "being abandoned by America in the face of the relentless advancement of European Islamization."

Maybe the center-right *Times of London* says it best. In an article titled "Eventually, We Will All Hate Obama Too," the paper predicts: "So Barack Obama, en fête [being celebrated] around the world, will one day learn that there is no magical cure for the envy of others. What makes America the indispensable power (and even more indispensable in the era of the new China), is precisely what makes anti-Americanism inevitable."

8

Europeans Continue to Love President Obama Despite His Policies

Gary Younge

Gary Younge is a feature writer and columnist for the Guardian.

Europeans disliked George W. Bush, but were very enthusiastic about the election of Barack Obama. Yet Barack Obama continued many of the policies Europeans disliked, including wars in Iraq and Afghanistan. Nevertheless, Obama's popularity remains high in Europe. This is because Europe itself, following a serious financial crisis, is weak, and because Europeans are so disgusted with their own leaders. Obama's popularity says less about his policies than it does about Europe's desperation.

In his book *Audacity of Hope*, [President] Barack Obama described himself as a Rorschach test—the famous psychological experiment where people are shown a series of ink blots and asked to identify what they see in them. There is no right answer. But each response in its own way, is thought to reveal the patient's obsessions and anxieties.

A Blank Screen

So it is with Obama. In the last week he has been disparaged as the "most successful food stamp president in history" by [former Republican speaker of the House] Newt Gingrich and a spineless "black mascot" of Wall Street by the prominent black academic Cornel West.

"I serve as a blank screen on which people of vastly different political stripes project their own views," he said. "As such I am bound to disappoint some if not all of them."

But one of the most curious things about those who support him most is not their disappointments—given their high hopes for him, that's to be expected—but their enduring devotion in the face of those disappointments. It's as though each single disillusionment is consumed as its own discrete letdown. String them together and you have not a narrative of failing to deliver on promises, but a litany of isolated, separate chapters—each with its own caveats, exceptions and explanations.

A Pew research poll published in July 2008, before the elections, revealed that Obama was more popular in Europe than any other continent, including North America.

This has long been true of black voters in the US, who somehow manage to feel more optimistic about America than ever, even as they are doing worse in it. Unemployment, poverty and foreclosure rates have risen to rates far higher than under George Bush, and the gap in opportunities between blacks and whites increases. Nonetheless, black Americans remain Obama's most loyal base. They are suffering from 16% unemployment, but they continue to give him 80% approval.

The same apparent contradictions underpin European attitudes to Obama, which have barely changed since his emergence as a credible presidential candidate. A Pew research poll published in July 2008, before the elections, revealed that Obama was more popular in Europe than any other continent, including North America.

In Germany, France, Spain and Britain, more than 70% said they trusted Obama "to do the right thing in world affairs" and more than half believed a new president would change US foreign policy for the better. While just 19% of Europeans interviewed in a German Marshall Fund survey in 2008 supported Bush's handling of international affairs, 77% approved of Obama's foreign policy a year later.

In September 2009 Craig Kennedy, the fund's president, argued: "I suspect that, as real political decisions have to be made, we will see 'Obama euphoria' fade as the Europeans begin to see him more as an American and less like themselves." But that hasn't happened. Three years later he leaves home—where, even after [terrorist leader] Osama bin Laden's assassination, approval ratings hover around 50%—and lands in a continent where more than 70% think he's doing a good job.

Obama and Bush

The strange thing is that much of what Europeans loathed about the Bush era remains intact even as Obama prepares to run for a second term Guantánamo [an American prison for terrorists in Cuba] is still open, rendition [the giving of terrorist suspects to regimes which may torture them] continues, there are more troops in Afghanistan and still troops in Iraq.

This could be overstated. Obama's statement on the Middle East last Friday [May 2011] shifts US policy on the region closer to Europe's than it has been for more than a decade. But that wouldn't be the first time he's delivered an impressive speech and then failed to follow through.

Moreover, Europe is implicated in many of the areas where foreign policy has stalled. Part of the problem with Guantánamo is that European governments refused to take many of the prisoners. Some applauded America's intensification of the war in Afghanistan even as they planned to unilaterally draw down their own troops.

"The problem is he's asking for roughly the same things President Bush asked for and President Bush didn't get them, not because he was a boorish diplomat or a cowboy," Peter Feaver, a former adviser to Bush now at Duke University, told the *New York Times* in 2009. "If that were the case, bringing in the sophisticated, urbane President Obama would have solved the problem. President Bush didn't get them because these countries had good reasons for not giving them."

Either way, Obama's principal defence abroad, as it is at home, is that things were bad when he arrived and would be worse if he went. This is true. But it falls far short of the inspiring rhetoric that accompanied his rise to power. Not so much "Yes we can" as "Could be worse".

Europeans don't just love Obama more than Americans do. They love him more than they love the people they have elected themselves.

Europe's Weak Leadership

European political elites have long been frustrated. "Maybe this is an overstatement, but I see this [European tour] as an opportunity for a reset of the European relationship," Heather Conley, director of the Europe programme at the Centre for Strategic and International Studies, told the *Washington Post*. "European leaders have really been struggling with where they fit. They had enormous expectations for this president, but they're now wondering, 'Is it that different after all?'"

But this has yet to filter down in any discernible way. So when he has delivered so little, why do Europeans love him so much? Many of the original reasons still stand. He still isn't George Bush, although how long that negative qualification remains meaningful is a moot point. He also emerged at a moment when European political leadership has been in a particularly parlous state. Europeans don't just love Obama more than Americans do. They love him more than they love the people they have elected themselves. One reason Obama is so popular in Europe is partly because he has emerged at a time when European leadership is in such a parlous state. Less than a third of the Italians and French, respectively, approve of [Italian Prime Minister] Silvio Berlusconi and [French President] Nicolas Sarkozy, only half the Germans find [German Prime Minister] Angela Merkel credible. [British Prime Minister] David Cameron does not fare much better.

Smart, charismatic, telegenic and unencumbered by sleaze Obama still, by comparison, represents the possibility of a popular form of electoral politics led by intelligent and public-spirited citizens as opposed to opportunists, egomaniacs and sleazemongers. It's as though his proven ability to articulate the source and scope of problems has enabled some people to look past his inability to provide a solution for them.

But in many ways Europe's Obamaphilia has always been as much a reflection of its weaknesses as his strengths. Like royalists in search of a benevolent monarch in whom they could invest great hopes but over whom they had no democratic control, they have sought not to leverage their own power but instead to trust in somebody else's.

And those weaknesses have grown. In the continuing fallout of the financial crisis, the continent is struggling to keep itself together. Greece and Ireland are on the brink of default, Portugal is up for a bailout and Spain is in revolt. The fate of the euro has been openly questioned.

And while many of the problems that dogged transatlantic relationships remain, almost everything else has changed. The Arab spring [in which numerous Arab countries revolted against dictatorial regimes] laid bare both the US's and Europe's waning influence on the world, while demands to retain the chairmanship of the IMF [International Monetary Fund] smack of anachronistic entitlement against the rising power of more dynamic developing economies.

European's attitudes towards Obama tell us more about Europe than they do about the US president. And what they say about both is not particularly impressive.

9

Anti-American Populism in Latin America Is Caused by US Policies

Justin Lance

Justin Lance is an instructor and graduate student at Ohio State University.

Populism is a political strategy that avoids traditional forms of organization, such as political parties, in favor of direct appeal to the public. There is no automatic connection between populism and anti-Americanism. However, America's policies towards Latin America have made anti-Americanism widespread in the region. These policies have included support for authoritarian regimes and support for neoliberal, or market-based, economic policies that are seen as causing great hardship and inequality. Thus, leaders like Venezuela's Hugo Chávez have been able to create populist movements by appealing in part to the public's intense dislike of the American government.

During President Bush's most recent trip to Latin America (in March of 2007), Venezuelan President Hugo Chávez launched what many called a counter-trip. Following President Bush's route in the region almost exactly, Chávez, an anti-American populist, called on Latin America to stand-up to what he sees as imperial U.S. policy towards the region and adopt what he calls his socialist alternative. Peppering his speeches with anti-American rhetoric, including condescending expletive phrases directed at U.S. government officials, Chávez is emblematic of a new type of leader in the region; the anti-American populist, that has attracted the attention of an increasing number of policymakers, scholars, and journalists (even Barbara Walters of ABC News interviewed Chávez recently).

Populism and Anti-Americanism Defined

While Chávez is the most emblematic of these leaders, and receives the bulk of media attention, the phenomenon is not unique to Venezuela. The presidents of Bolivia and Ecuador as well as the leading left-wing candidate in Mexico's most recent presidential election have run populist campaigns, and the former have governed in a populist style. This [viewpoint] briefly outlines why populism and anti-Americanism are important, what they are specifically, and what conditions have led to their reemergence today.

To begin it is important to note what populism is, what anti-Americanism is, and how the two terms are related. Populism is a very broad term and, often evokes negative connotations. It suggests a pre-democratic way of governing, though its meaning in practice is often fuzzy and contested. For example, populism is often associated with economic redistribution and socialism, social equality, and some forms of nationalism. While this may be the case in practice, as discussed below, not all socialists or leftists, social activists, or nationalists are populists. For instance, many politicians on the left in Latin America today, such as the current Presidents of Brazil and Chile, are *not* populists.

Consequently, the most common definition of populism in political science today considers populism as a distinct political strategy where a personalistic leader tries to capture the vote of previously unorganized voters by shunning and/or outright disparaging existing institutions, by speaking directly to "the people."

In other words, populism is a way of competing in elections and governing once in office that largely eschews traditional forms of organization, particularly political parties, in favor of direct contact with a newly organized political mass.

Unlike populism, anti-Americanism is better understood. Anti-Americanism refers primarily to negative feelings or attitudes towards the United States government and, in rare occasions, its citizens. Therefore, *By definition* populism and anti-Americanism are somewhat unrelated. *In practice*, however, they are often closely linked, a relationship which began with the first wave of populism in Latin America from the 1930s until the 1950s, as discussed below.

Traditional Populism: A Return to the Past

Traditional populists—such as Juan Peron in Argentina (1946–1955, 1973–1974), Getulio Vargas in Brazil (1930–1945, 1950–1954), and Lázaro Cárdenas in Mexico (1934–1940)—were nationalists who bypassed the traditional ruling elite and formed new movements of previously nonexistent voters. They captured a large part of the vote by appealing to new masses of urban industrial workers—a societal group that had formed in response to state intervention in the economy. The roots of populist anti-Americanism grew during this period as the state created government-run industries that resulted in a large industrial and unionized middle class.

The programs of state intervention were particularly key to building domestic economic independence since, until this time, Latin American economies had been reliant upon American companies, and international economic activity was based almost entirely on exporting raw material goods (such as fruit, coffee, and beef) to the United States and Europe.

The populist politicians were able to capture the votes of this new social group in three ways: by distancing themselves from the old parties associated with the elite, wealthy classes of society; by acting as if they were speaking directly to voters; and by promising to implement social security, wage, and food programs that would benefit the new urban, industrial worker. Part of the reason for the popularity of populist politicians stemmed from the perceived need for these programs from many in this group. Anti-Americanism also grew during this period since most of these leaders were nationalists.

Many dictators . . . came to power with the assistance of the United States, and the U.S. helped to fund a number of dictatorships through aid programs.

Traditional populism came to end when the military took over in many Latin American countries starting in the 1960s. Although many older populists were part of the military (Juan Peron, for example, was a military officer), the new military leaders drew from more conservative elements of society.

They also enjoyed the support of the United States, which attempted to counter increasing communist and Soviet influence in the region by backing brutal military regimes, including that of Augosto Pinochet, discussed below. This support would later become a leading source of anti-Americanism in the region upon which modern populists have been able to build (in conjunction with other factors). Many dictators, like Pinochet, came to power with the assistance of the United States, and the U.S. helped to fund a number of dictatorships through aid programs.

Two factors led to the end of the traditional populist period. First, the military had eliminated many of the traditional supporters of populism, either through exile or violent means. For example, during military rule in Argentina, the military crackdown targeted some Peron supporters, including trade union leaders, students, and others on the left in what was known as "the Dirty War." Estimates are that over 30,000 people "disappeared" during this period (most likely killed by the military that dropped their bodies in the shark infested ocean). Furthermore, declassified US documents suggest, as many suspected, that the US was well aware of what was going on and even encouraged the Argentine military action.

Anti-Americanism has its roots not necessarily in populism, but rather the United States' intervention in the Latin American region.

Second, it was assumed that during the re-democratization process that began in the 1980s, countries would begin to develop political institutions (and, in turn, political leaders) that resembled the developed world. Many policymakers thought that Latin American countries would develop political institutions that would prevent populism from reappearing. However, this was not the case, and in conjunction with market-oriented economic reform, the seeds of resurgent populism and anti-Americanism were sown.

The Historical Basis for Anti-Americanism

Anti-Americanism has its roots not necessarily in populism, but rather the United States' intervention in the Latin American region. Since the Monroe Doctrine, [a U.S. policy that said the U.S. would not tolerate European interference in the western hemisphere] particularly before 9/11, the United States considered the Western Hemisphere to be its *domaine reserve* meaning that no other country should mess in the United States' "backyard." The U.S. had routinely intervened in Mexico during the late 1800 and early 1900s, and the U.S. led invasion of Cuba in 1898 (the Spanish-American War) set up a proxy state sympathetic to U.S. interests.

The purpose of these interventions was during the post-colonial period (from the 1830s until the 1930s), was often to secure access to raw materials for U.S. companies. U.S. companies had unparalleled access to the region and often operated with impunity with regard to the local population. Large U.S.-based corporations—such as Folgers and the United Fruit Company (now Chiquita)—operated much like independent states throughout the region while exporting raw materials to the United States and Europe. These corporations' actions, sometimes violent, were among those that helped the nationalist populists who advocated more state control of the economy and a domestically oriented perspective on economic development.

Instead of exporting raw materials and importing manufactured goods, these countries focused their attention on their own economies to limit the amount of foreign goods imported into their countries by creating domestic industries to produce manufactured goods.

The United States also supported military leaders, discussed above, who were vehemently anti-communist. The Cold War dimension pitted many on the left against the United States and conservative military elements of society.

U.S. overt and covert support for these regimes was a leading cause of anti-Americanism for those on the left. Concerned about Soviet advances in the region after the Cuban Revolution, U.S. interventions in Guatemala, Cuba and the Dominican Republic were viewed with hostility among many in the region. Plans like Operation Condor, where the U.S. and allied Latin American governments sought to kill Marxists and leftists in the region, and U.S. covert support for the military coup of Augusto Pinochet against the only democratically elected Marxist head of state, Salvador Allende, led many on the left toward an increasingly anti-American position.

Pinochet's regime is often considered to have been more brutal than the Argentine military regime discussed above; at one point in time, the Soviet Union (not known for its respect for human rights) even refused to play a World Cup qualifying game in the National Stadium since it was used as a detention and torture center for dissidents of the Pinochet regime!

A final dimension leading to anti-Americanism appeared in the mid-1980s and 1990s in the form of U.S. support for economic reform programs. As mentioned earlier, Latin American countries had from the 1930's on industrialized products by relying on economic intervention by the government, a process known as "import substitution industrialization." ISI did indeed help to industrialize many Latin American economies, but it came with a price: mounting debt caused by high borrowing.

By the 1980s, the situation had reached a climax, resulting in the 1982 debt crisis in which a number of Latin American countries defaulted on their loans and entered a period of economic distress. In fact, these economic woes earned the 1980s the title of "the Lost Decade" by many Latin Americans.

The solution to these problems proposed (and considered by some to be imposed) by the U.S., International Monetary Fund (IMF), and World Bank was a series of reforms to remove state intervention from the economy and adopt market economic principles. State-run companies were sold, tariff barriers dropped, and foreign investment encouraged among other reform measures. Strong U.S. support for these reforms (often called neo-liberalism) has become a primary source of anti-Americanism today.

Sources of Anti-Americanism and Populism Today

While military interventions, economic exploitation, and covert U.S. political and economic support for brutal military regimes provide the historical foundations for anti-Americanism and populism, a confluence of more recent events explains why the resurgence has happened now. We can point to five which have fueled the rise of anti-American populism:

1. The failure of neoliberal economic reform to benefit large sectors of these societies and worsening economic inequality

2. Weak, corrupt political institutions

3. U.S. immigration policy, especially toward Mexico and Central America

4. U.S.-led intervention of Iraq in 2003

5. The continuing hegemonic position of the United States in relation to the region culturally, economically, and politically

Neoliberalism has often been perceived as one of the causes for increasing economic inequality in the region.

These conditions have led a larger number of people, particularly poor voters who feel disenfranchised by the current political system, to begin supporting politicians such as Hugo Chávez in Venezuela, Evo Morales in Bolivia, Rafael Correa in Ecuador, and Andrés Manuel López Obrador in Mexico. These politicians often used populist political strategies when campaigning, and routinely critiqued U.S. supported economic policies, immigration policy, and U.S. unilateralism when campaigning.

The first condition has been a proximate cause for both anti-Americanism and populist politicians who promise economic redistribution of wealth. Neoliberalism [that is, strongly Pro-market economic policies] has often been perceived as one of the causes for increasing economic inequality in the region. Latin America generally has one of the most lopsided wealth distributions in the world. The richest 10% of the population earns 47% of the income in the region, while the poorest 10% accounts for just 2–4% of the income, making Latin America vastly more unequal than the developed nations, eastern Europe, most of Asia, and even parts of Africa.

Politicians have been able to capitalize on this economic divide by promising to rapidly redistribute wealth to the poor. This has thus been a primary source of anti-Americanism because the U.S. strongly supported these neoliberal economic reforms that many feel has failed to remedy long-term economic problems.

In Latin America ... corrupt parties and weak political structures ... give populists the opportunity not only to compete in elections, but also the ability to win them.

Weak Institutions

The second condition is related to the ability of populists to win political office. Weak and ineffective political institutions, in particular political parties, give populist politicians the chance to effectively win office in Latin America. While populists exist elsewhere (in the U.S. Ross Perot and Ralph Nader could be considered populist politicians), the possibility for winning office is greatly diminished by the political institutions of these countries. The U.S. system, in particular, has a number of laws that prevent new parties from winning elections.

In Latin America, however, corrupt parties and weak political structures that make populist parties and politicians viable candidates, gives populists the opportunity not only to compete in elections, but also the ability to win them. Many of the poor feel slighted by the traditional ruling elites, who are often accused of corruption and nepotism.

Populists, distancing themselves from the traditional ruling elite, have been able to capture a large number of poor voters who feel disenfranchised by the other political parties. What concerns most scholars and policymakers is the anti-system approach taken by many populists.

The third, fourth and fifth conditions also help to account for a rise in anti-Americanism in the region. The third condition is a prominent reason for anti-Americanism in Mexico and Central America, which have higher emigration rates to the U.S. in comparison to countries in South America. The increasing salience of immigration policy in the U.S.—as well as the perception that immigrants from Latin America are illegal and treated as second class citizens (or non-citizens altogether) in the U.S.—has led many citizens in countries with high emigration rates to be concerned (and critical) about U.S. immigration policies.

The fourth condition has led to decreasing support for U.S. foreign policy, especially in South American countries. . . . Recent survey research suggests that perceptions of the United States have declined since the start of the Iraq War. These attitudes can be attributed to increasing concern about the U.S. policy to "go it alone" in Iraq and its unwillingness to consult allies during times of turmoil. Latin Americans also perceive (and, often rightly so) that their region has declined in importance to U.S. foreign policy in the post-9/11 world. Traditionally the most important region for the United States abroad, Latin America has seen a steady decline in importance in a world in which terrorism takes center-stage.

It should be noted, however, that anti-American hostility is directed largely at the U.S. government—not toward U.S. citizens more generally. . . . Many hold an unfavorable opinion of President Bush at both the elite and mass level. But many Latin Americans across the region also hold a similarly unfavorable opinion of Hugo Chávez, the most anti-American populist in region.

Importantly, survey research on the final condition disaggregates opinions on anti-Americanism between elites and the masses. In fact, many citizens draw a distinction between the U.S. government and American culture. . . . Many in the region admire aspects of American culture but are still concerned about their spread. Interestingly, the country most supportive of U.S. culture is also the country with the most anti-American populist in power (Venezuela). Other countries, such as Argentina, are considerably more skeptical of U.S. cultural influence.

Chavéz' support tends to be drawn from the lower classes, academics, and leftists, and he has promised to radically redistribute Venezuela's vast oil wealth to the poorer segments of society.

The Anti-American Populist Today

The conditions that have led to anti-Americanism and populism today are best seen in the career of Venezuelan President Hugo Chávez. Chávez regularly [condemns] U.S. actions abroad and is very critical, even derogatory at times, toward the Bush administration. Chávez' support tends to be drawn from the lower classes, academics, and leftists, and he has promised to radically redistribute Venezuela's vast oil wealth to the poorer segments of society.

Chávez often follows the path of the populist politician, holding a regularly scheduled, three-hour presidential news broadcast (called Aló Presidente) during which he "speaks directly with the people." Recent wins by his party of all the seats in Congress (due to the opposition parties pulling out) and Congressional approval for Chávez to pass legislation by decree without congressional approval has led to increasing criticism that he is a dictator and not a democrat. Only time will tell whether Chávez will become more of a democrat or more of a dictator.

The nationalist foundation of populism and anti-Americanism directed toward market reforms has also led to new ways of organizing the economy. In Venezuela and Bolivia (under populist politician Evo Morales), a new round of nationalization (or the purchase of private companies by the state) has occurred. While both countries have paid for their acquisitions, many—particularly those in the U.S. business community, U.S. government, and IMF—have been concerned about these recent trends.

There have also been political changes associated this new type of politician. Most, including Chávez, Morales, and Ecuador's populist president Rafael Correa, have sought to reorganize the constitutions of their respective countries to grant the poor or indigenous inhabitants (in the cases of Ecuador and Bolivia) more political powers. These groups, traditionally slighted by the ruling elite, certainly have cause for optimism in the region.

There have also been setbacks. Populist politicians recently lost elections in Peru and Mexico, and there have been signs that some populists in office are following a more "regular" path than initially anticipated. The historical dimension is clear, however: it is often only with violence that the populist politician can be thrown out. What this holds for the future of democracy in Latin America is unclear; as Latin America enters what is often a difficult period for new democracies, only time will tell about the impact of populism on Latin American political systems.

10

America's Policies Have Made Libya Love America and Its Pop Culture

David Zucchino

David Zucchino is a foreign correspondent for the Los Angeles Times.

The United States has provided important support to Libyan rebels fighting to overthrow dictator Moammar Kadafi. In large part as a result, America itself and American cultural products have become hugely popular in Libya, especially among the Libyan resistance. The American flag in particular is often carried at resistance rallies. Libyans say that they see the American flag as a symbol of the freedoms that Libyans hope to secure for themselves.

Omar el Keish wanted to make a strong statement when he headed out with his wife and daughter recently for a revolutionary rally here [Benghazi, Libya] in the de facto rebel capital.

Taking the Flag

Keish decided to bring along a flag. It wasn't the ubiquitous Libyan rebel flag that flutters at every downtown rally. He chose the American flag—the Stars and Stripes—on a long, heavy pole.

The 57-year-old airline pilot waved the big fluttering fabric with both arms, and rallygoers smiled and flashed the V for victory sign at the sight of Old Glory.

"Libyans love America," Keish explained as he cut through a boisterous crowd that numbered in the tens of thousands. "They love the flag because it stands for freedom and democracy—exactly what they want for Libya."

In a region where America is often mistrusted and resented, rebel-held eastern Libya stands out as an island of pro-American sentiment. The ragtag forces that drove out [Libyan dictator] Moammar Kadafi's security forces in February [2011] credit U.S. and NATO warplanes for rescuing Benghazi from a government counterattack in March.

America's popularity has risen further since July 15, when the U.S. formally recognized the rebel Transitional National Council as the sole legitimate representative of the Libyan people.

More American flags have begun to pop up at opposition rallies and outside shops. Some young men sport ball caps emblazoned with a small U.S. flag and the New York Yankees logo.

Anti-Kadafi graffiti that dominates the Benghazi cityscape occasionally includes the American flag or pro-U.S. slogans. Schoolchildren occasionally place the Stars and Stripes in their anti-Kadafi drawings.

"I made a whole new supply of American flags after the U.S. recognition, and I've sold most of them already," said Mohammed Ali Harari, a tailor who sews and sells foreign flags at the Benghazi courthouse complex.

Not that the United States is the most popular foreign country here. That designation is shared by France and Qatar, which have provided the rebels with weapons as well as money and political support. Some rebel fighters fly the French tricolor on their gun trucks and several downtown buildings sport the maroon-and-white Qatari flag alongside the red-black-and-green rebel flag.

The U.S., for its part, has provided $25 million in nonlethal military aid to the rebels, including uniforms and ready-to-eat halal [permissable under Islamic law] meals. Some members of Congress have suggested providing weapons, but the Obama administration has ruled that out so far.

Still, many Libyans consider the U.S. the sole foreign power capable of toppling Kadafi. For that reason, Kadafi's opponents tend to praise U.S. policy toward Libya while also expressing frustration that America has not done more.

Young volunteers at the front, in particular, say their patience is running out. They contend that the United States could overthrow Kadafi but is holding back.

If U.S. policy is generally admired here, America's cultural appeal is off the charts.

"We expect more from America—they're the most powerful country, and they can do anything," said Ali Abdelsalam, 27, an electronics salesman. "They have the best weapons. They should give them to us, and then we could finish Kadafi right now."

Everything American

If U.S. policy is generally admired here, America's cultural appeal is off the charts. American websites, cellphones, videos, music, clothing, cars and movies are immensely popular among the young men who form the core of the rebels' volunteer force. American pop culture is also popular in Arab countries less enamored of U.S. policy.

Perhaps the single-most coveted status symbol here is the iPhone. Imported from Dubai or Europe, it sells for about 1,400 Libyan dinars, or $1,090, here. Young men save for months for one, and many beg friends traveling to Europe, where iPhones cost less, to bring back one for them.

Young men also spend exorbitant amounts for Nike sneakers. Wealthy Libyans cruise Benghazi in imported Hummers and Ford Mustangs—drawing envious stares from men lounging at cafes.

Car radios blast American rap music—Jay-Z, 50 Cent and Eminem. Satellite TV channels from Egypt and Dubai, United Arab Emirates, broadcast mainstream American standards such as "The Oprah Winfrey Show," "Lost," "Friends," "Prison Break" and "Pimp My Ride."

Young Libyans, who watch KFC and McDonald's ads on foreign satellite channels, complain that the fast food isn't available here. But restaurants offer "beef burgers" ("hamburger" sounds too much like a pork product), and diners who want fried chicken order "Kentucky chicken."

English usage is surprisingly widespread among rebel fighters at the front. Gunmen often tell visiting American journalists that they want to emigrate to the United States—after they topple Kadafi.

"Thank you America!" Yousif Abuleifa, 31, an oil engineer who has volunteered at the front, hollered at an American reporter who was chatting with Keish, the flag-waving pilot.

"We know we couldn't have faced down this dictator without America's support—France and the UK, too, but especially America," Abuleifa said, pointing to Keish's flag.

Keish said he lived in Southern California from 1976 to 1990, working as a flight instructor at John Wayne Airport in Santa Ana. He said he's proud to be Libyan—especially an anti-Kadafi Libyan—but admires the freedoms and choices available in the United States.

"That's why I fly the flag—to support American-style freedoms that we all want here," he said.

Harari, the flag-making tailor, said it wasn't difficult to create copies of American flags he'd seen on TV. He's made three sizes, selling them from $23 to $39.

The biggest ones have 50 stars and 13 stripes. But the popular small flags feature, for reasons Harari could not explain, 70 stars and 15 stripes.

"They just want the flag," he said, shrugging. "They don't care how many stars it has."

11

Love of American Pop Culture Counteracts Anti-Americanism Worldwide

Ioannis Gatsiounis

Ioannis Gatsiounis is a writer and foreign correspondent based in Malaysia.

Anti-Americanism abroad has increased during the George W. Bush administration. At the same time, however, Hollywood movies abroad have increased in popularity. People in other countries may enjoy Hollywood films in part because they show things foreigners claim not to like, but are actually fascinated by. The popularity of Hollywood film helps counteract negative stereotypes of America and American culture.

President [George W.] Bush's foreign policy is said to have unleashed an intense and potentially irreversible strain of anti-Americanism around the world, one in which the line between hating American leaders and culture is blurring.

International Success

And yet Hollywood, a symbol of US "hegemony" if ever there was one, is appreciating greater success abroad than at home. International ticket sales now account for 60 percent of overall box office receipts, up from 40 percent three years ago. Home-video sales are said to be the fastest-growing revenue sector in

Tinseltown, and that doesn't include the millions watching pirated copies. Meanwhile American television shows attract a record number of foreign program buyers, even though licensing fees have increased sharply in most markets.

So what gives?

Part of the answer lies in trade liberalization. Part rests with shrewder, more global-minded marketing. Major studios are beefing up their overseas divisions and signing foreign partnerships. Warner Bros., for instance, recently penned a $2 billion deal with Abu Dhabi's largest real-estate firm, Aldar, to build a studio and produce films and videogames—thus targeting the Arab world, 60 percent of which is under 25 and regarded as entertainment hungry.

Lower labor costs and fewer regulations also inspire moves abroad. Major Hollywood studios set up production houses in China, to better tap growing interest in films. Hollywood's production costs decreased in 2005 by 4 percent while marketing costs jumped 5.2 percent.

The industry has always welcomed international talent, from [German actor] Marlene Dietrich to [Scottish actor] Sean Connery, but as Hollywood pushes its product aggressively abroad, executives view international talent as ever more critical in promoting films abroad.

In "The Kingdom" Jamie Foxx stars beside Palestinian actor Ashraf Barhom, who plays a brave Saudi Arabian police officer. "The Last Samurai" stars Tom Cruise and Japanese actor Ken Watanabe, scoring well in Japan. Brazilian actress Alice Braga joins Will Smith in "I Am Legend." Hollywood tackles transnational hot topics like religion ("Kingdom of Heaven"), terrorism ("Munich"), deadly viruses ("I Am Legend") and the oil trade ("Syriana").

In short, Hollywood is thinking bigger and bigger—with no less than the world in mind.

Policies and Values

But none of this sufficiently explains why Hollywood enjoys unprecedented success abroad in an era of rampant American-bashing. The common explanation for the contradiction has been that the world makes a distinction between American culture and its foreign policy; that the more sweeping variety of anti-Americanism is confined mostly to intellectuals and religious zealots.

Typical "all-American" fare plays well in international theaters.

But over the last few years in Europe and Asia I've encountered more ordinary citizens baldly denouncing America. It is not just America's politics, they carp, but "hypocritical" values, a "hollow" pop culture and disbelief about voters re-electing Bush. A poll from the Pew Global Attitudes Project supports such anecdotal evidence, finding that favorable opinions of American people among Indonesians dropped from 56 percent in 2002 to 46 percent in 2005, and also fell in Great Britain, Poland, Canada, Germany, France, Russia, Jordan, Turkey and Pakistan. To be sure Bush's foreign policy and his successful reelection bid precipitated a broader disdain for America, and that makes Hollywood's growth abroad all the more noteworthy.

Still, typical "all-American" fare plays well in international theaters. "Spider-Man 3" was the biggest worldwide opener in history, raking in $375 million. "The Simpsons Movie," featuring "America's first family," grossed nearly $333 million abroad, double what it did stateside. Hollywood's most successful titles abroad tend to be special effect-heavy ("Titanic," "Harry Potter," "Pirates of the Caribbean" "Jurassic Park") and animation and digital wizardry ("Shrek" "The Lion King" and "The Incredibles"). Ironically perhaps these films tend to do better than those critical of the US, such as "Fahrenheit 9/11," "Syriana" and "American Beauty." Moo Hon Mei, marketing director for Twentieth Century Fox Malaysia, said this trend has remained largely undisturbed in Southeast Asia over the years and "doesn't look set to change anytime soon."

Either way, viewers of Hollywood pictures are hard pressed to ignore that they are invested in an American product—the American flag here, the country's natural splendor there. Hollywood tendentiously celebrates America's unique brand of dynamism, from its confidence and cool to its technological and creative preeminence.

And generally people like what they see, a fact reflected not only in the numbers Hollywood posts, but in official backlash and its impact. In December, China banned the release of US films for at least three months. The success of American films at the expense of local fare is said to have influenced the decision. South Korea relies on a quota that requires local films to play 146 days of the year, a number halved as part of the US-Korea bilateral trade agreement, yet to be ratified.

Fascinated with America

In March Javad Shangari, a cultural adviser to Iranian President Mahmoud Ahmadinejad, accused Hollywood of being "part of a comprehensive U.S. psychological war aimed at Iranian culture," in response to the film "300," which some critics suggested was anti-Persian. A government spokesperson added "Cultural intrusion is among the tactics always used by the aliens."

In Malaysia, authorities barred moviegoers from Mel Gibson's "The Passion of the Christ," to protect Muslim "sensitivities," but pirated versions were readily available at stalls around Kuala Lumpur. China's street corners are rife with pirated Hollywood movies, and young Iranians adore American films, often edited or banned.

Hollywood's portrayals of America as a den of iniquity may even feed some misconceptions. In the Pew poll more than 60 percent of Lebanese describe Americans as greedy, violent and immoral, yet Lebanon is one of Hollywood's hottest markets in the Middle East. The fact that Hollywood is a hit in such places signals, at the least, a healthy fascination with the "depravity" of America and, more likely, a gap between what people say and what they actually think about the country. A young Malaysian woman accounted for complexity in her relationship with the US when she articulated her affinity for Hollywood in broad terms, saying that it enabled her "to imagine doing things not practiced or accepted at home."

With anti-Americanism reaching record highs, Hollywood is not only a powerful ideological tool, but arguably a necessary one.

Hollywood doesn't specialize in just "sin," and audiences do not merely line up for a peek at sin. "[Hollywood] allows people abroad to learn about American society and especially affluence, fashions, consumption patterns, etc., that people are interested in, never mind their anti-American attitudes," said Paul Hollander, editor of the essay collection "Understanding Anti-Americanism."

Edward Said lamented US power in this respect, that is, ideological power: "All cultures tend to make representations of foreign cultures . . . to master or in some way control them. Yet not all cultures make representations of foreign cultures and in fact master or control them." . . .

With anti-Americanism reaching record highs, Hollywood is not only a powerful ideological tool, but arguably a necessary one. The success of Al Gore's "An Inconvenient Truth," for instance, reminded the world that, yes, some US politicians genuinely have the world's interest at heart.

Hollywood's "window" complicates the world's relationship with the US. It challenges the malicious simplifications of American politics and culture, inculcated through politically motivated critics, religious institutions, governments, schools and media.

In doing so, Hollywood challenges the impulse to dismiss and demonize, and in our polarizing world it could do much worse.

Organizations to Contact

The editors have compiled the following list of organizations concerned with the issues debated in this book. The descriptions are derived from materials provided by the organizations. All have publications or information available for interested readers. The list was compiled on the date of publication of the present volume; the information provided here may change. Be aware that many organizations take several weeks or longer to respond to inquiries, so allow as much time as possible.

ACT! for America
PO Box 12765, Pensacola, FL   32591
e-mail: info@actforamerica.org
website: www.actforamerica.org/

ACT! for America is a nonpartisan, non-sectarian organization devoted to educating Americans about the threat of radical Islam. It advances this goal through grassroots organizing and lobbying, and through creating a nationwide network of chapters to inform, educate, and mobilize Americans. Its website includes news announcements, video discussions, and information about chapters and initiatives.

Americans for Middle East Understanding (AMEU)
475 Riverside Dr., Room 245, New York, NY   10115
(212) 870-2053 • fax: (212) 870-2050
e-mail: info@ameu.org
website: www.ameu.org

Americans for Middle East Understanding (AMEU) is an organization founded to foster a better understanding in America of the history, goals, and values of Middle Eastern cultures and peoples, the rights of Palestinians, and the forces shaping US policy in the Middle East. AMEU publishes *The Link*, a bimonthly newsletter, as well as books and pamphlets on the Middle East.

The Brookings Institution

1775 Massachusetts Ave. NW, Washington, DC   20036
(202) 797-6000
e-mail: communications@brookings.edu
website: www.brookings.edu

The Brookings Institution, founded in 1927, is a liberal think tank that conducts research and education in foreign policy, economics, government, and the social sciences. It publishes numerous books and the quarterly *Brookings Review*. Its website includes numerous papers and articles, including "The Anatomy of Anti-Americanism in Turkey" and "Anti-Americanism and Ambivalence in the New Germany."

Carnegie Endowment for International Peace (CEIP)

1779 Massachusetts Ave. NW, Washington, DC   20036
(202) 483-7600 • fax: (202) 483-1840
e-mail: info@carnegieendowment.org
website: www.carnegieendowment.org

The Carnegie Endowment for International Peace (CEIP) is a private, nonprofit organization dedicated to advancing cooperation between nations and promoting active international engagement by the United States. It publishes the quarterly journal *Foreign Policy*, a magazine of international politics and economics that is published in several languages and reaches readers in more than 120 countries. Its website includes numerous news articles and publications, such as "American NGOs and US-Egypt Relations," and "Yes, the Afghans Hate Us."

Cato Institute

1000 Massachusetts Ave. NW, Washington, DC   20001
(202) 842-0200 • fax (202) 842-3490
website: www.cato.org

The Cato Institute is a libertarian public policy research foundation dedicated to increasing the understanding of public policies based on the principles of limited government, free markets, individual liberty, and peace. It is generally opposed to American interventions abroad. It publishes the triannual *Cato Journal*, the periodic *Cato Policy Analysis*, and a bi-monthly newsletter, *Cato Policy Review*. The website also includes articles such as "The Dangers of European Anti-Americanism," and "Responding to Anti-Americanism in the Arab World."

Council on Foreign Relations

58 E. 68th St., New York, NY 10065
(212) 434-9400 • fax: (212) 434-9800
e-mail: communications@cfr.org
website: www.cfr.org

The Council on Foreign Relations researches the international aspects of American economic and political policies. Its journal *Foreign Affairs*, published five times a year, provides analysis on global conflicts. Articles on its website include "Pakistani Media and Anti-Americanism" and "The Real Roots of Arab Anti-Americanism."

The Heritage Foundation

214 Massachusetts Ave. NE, Washington, DC 20002
(202) 546-4400 • fax (202) 546-8328
e-mail: info@heritage.org
website: www.heritage.org

The Heritage Foundation is a research and educational institute that promotes conservative public policies based on the principles of free enterprise, limited government, individual freedom, traditional American values, and a strong national defense. Its website includes policy briefs and articles such as "Anti-Americanism in Pakistan: What Fuels It and How It Can Be Countered," and "Roots of Russian Anti-Americanism."

Hoover Institution

434 Galvez Mall, Stanford University, Stanford, CA 94305
(650) 723-1754 • fax: (650) 723-1687
website: www.hoover.org

The Hoover Institution is a public policy research center housed at Stanford University devoted to advanced study of politics, economics, and political economy—both domestic and foreign—as well as international affairs. It publishes a newsletter and the quarterly *Hoover Digest*. Its website includes articles such as "Anti-Americanism in Europe: A Cultural Problem," and "Confronting Anti-Americanism Abroad—and At Home."

Institute for Policy Studies
1112 16th St. NW, Suite 600, Washington, DC   20036
(202) 234-9382
e-mail: info@ips-dc.org
website: www.ips-dc.org

The goal of the Institute for Policy Studies is to empower people to build healthy and democratic societies in communities, the US, and around the world. The institute publishes a newsletter and also the magazine *Foreign Policy in Focus*, which offers briefings and reports on major developments in U.S. foreign policy. It also publishes books on foreign policy. Its website includes articles such as "The Roots of Muslim Anger At America" and "The U.S. As Global Outcast: Growing Anti-Americanism."

Pew Global Attitudes Project
1615 L Street NW, Suite 700, Washington, DC   20036
(202) 419-4300 • fax: (202) 419-4349
info@pewresearch.org
website: http://pewresearch.org

The Pew Research Center's Global Attitudes Project conducts public opinion surveys around the world on a broad array of subjects. It has conducted more than 270,000 interviews in 57 countries. Its website includes reports on its surveys such as "The American-Western European Values Gap" and "Muslim-Western Tensions Persist."

Bibliography

Books

David Blankenhorn, Abdou Filali-Ansary, Hassan I. Mneimneh, and Alex Roberts, eds.
The Islam/West Debate: Documents From a Global Debate on Terrorism, U.S. Policy, and the Middle East. Lanham, MD: Rowman & Littlefield Publishers, 2005.

Lane Crothers
Globalization and American Popular Culture, 2nd Edition. Lanham, MD: Rowman & Littlefield Publishers, 2009.

Brigitte Gabriel
They Must Be Stopped: Why We Must Defeat Radical Islam and How We Can Do It. New York, NY: St. Martin's Press, 2008.

John Gibson
Hating America: The New World Sport. New York: HarperCollins, 2004.

Stephen Glain
State Vs. Defense: The Battle to Define America's Empire. New York: Crown, 2011.

Paul Hollander
Understanding Anti-Americanism: Its Origins and Impact at Home and Abroad. Chicago, IL: Ivan R. Dee Publisher, 2004.

Richard H. Immerman   *Empire for Liberty: A History of American Imperialism from Benjamin Franklin to Paul Wolfowitz*. Princeton, NJ: Princeton University Press, 2010.

Peter J. Katzenstein and Robert O. Keohane, eds.   *Anti-Americanism in World Politics*. Ithaca, NY: Cornell University Press, 2006.

Jing Li   *China's America: The Chinese View of the United States, 1990–2000*. Albany, NY: State University of New York Press, 2011.

Alan McPherson   *Yankee No! Anti-Americanism in U.S.-Latin American Relations*. Cambridge, MA: Harvard University Press, 2003.

Barry Rubin and Judith Colp Rubin   *Hating America: A History*. New York, NY: Oxford University Press, 2004.

Glenn E. Schweitzer and Carole D. Schweitzer   *America on Notice: Stemming the Tide of Anti-Americanism*. Amherst, NY: Prometheus Books, 2006.

Nancy Snow   *Persuader-in-Chief: Global Opinion and Public Diplomacy in the Age of Obama*. Ann Arbor, MI: Nimble Books, 2009.

Wafa Sultan   *A God Who Hates: The Courageous
                   Woman Who Inflamed the Muslim
                   World Speaks Out Against the Evils of
                   Islam.* New York: St. Martin's Press,
                   2009.

Hal Weitzman   *Latin Lessons: How South America
                   Stopped Listening to the United States
                   and Started Prospering.* Hoboken, NJ:
                   John Wiley & Sons, 2012.

Periodicals and Internet Sources

Tim Arango   "World Falls For American Media,
                   Even As It Sours on America," *New
                   York Times*, November 30, 2008.

Allan J. Ashinoff "Why Islam Hates America,"
                   American Chronicle, July 25, 2005.
                   www.americanchronicle.com.

Bruce Bawer   "Hating America," *Hudson Review*,
                   Vol. 57, No. 1, Spring 2004.

BBC World   "Global Views of United States
Service   Improve While Other Countries
                   Decline," April 18, 2010.

Bernard Chazelle   "Anti-Americanism: A Clinical
                   Study," *Princeton University*,
                   September 2004. www.cs.princeton
                   .edu.

Michael Crowley   "Obama Fails to Budge Arab
                   Opinion," *Swampland—Time.com*,
                   July 14, 2011. http://swampland
                   .time.com.

Henry Farrell   "What Drives Anti-Americanism in Muslim Countries?" *The Monkey Cage*, February 28, 2011. http://themonkeycage.org.

Howard Fineman   "Post-Anti-Americanism: Europe Can't Even Be Bothered to Hate America Any More," *Newsweek*, August 9, 2010.

Thomas L. Friedman   "America vs. The Narrative," *New York Times*, November 28, 2009.

Neil Gross   "The Many Stripes of Anti-Americanism," *Boston Globe*, January 14, 2007.

Bridget Johnson   "Why the World Hates America," *PJ Media*, June 14, 2008. http://pjmedia.com.

Ying Ma   "China's America Problem," Hoover Institution, February 1, 2002. www.hoover.org.

Kenneth Maxwell   "Anti-Americanism in Brazil," Council on Foreign Relations, Spring 2002. www.cfr.org.

John McCain, Lindsey Graham, Mark Kirk, and Marco Rubio   "The Promise of a Pro-American Libya," *Wall Street Journal*, October 7, 2011.

John Nolte   "But-But-But Hollywood Told Me Pro-America Doesn't Sell Overseas," *Big Hollywood*, August 4, 2011. http://bighollywood.breitbart.com.

Stephen M. Walt   "Why They Hate Us (I): On Military
                         Occupation," *Foreign Policy*,
                         November 23, 2009. http://walt
                         .foreignpolicy.com.

Stephen M. Walt   "Why they Hate Us (II): How Many
                         Muslims Has the U.S. Killed in the
                         Past 30 Years?" *Foreign Policy*,
                         November 30, 2009. http://walt
                         .foreignpolicy.com.

Jonathan   "Hollywood and the Spread of
Wellemeyer   Anti-Americanism," NPR, December
                         20, 2006. www.npr.org.

Robert S.   "The Anti-Imperialism of Fools,"
Wistrich   *Israel National News*, March 11, 2010.
                         www.israelnationalnews.com.

Mark Zepezauer   "Why the Right Hates America,"
                         Counterpunch, February 28-March 1,
                         2003. www.counterpunch.org.

Index

A

Abdelsalam, Ali, 78

Abu Ghraib prison (Iraq), 42, 55

Abuleifa, Yousif, 79

Afghanistan
Soviet occupation, 32, 34–35
US invasion and war, 17, 19, 61

African-Americans, support for President Obama, 60

Ahmadinejad, Mahmoud, 47

al-Qaeda, 17, 35, 46, 47

Allende, Salvador, 69

Anti-Americanism
Arab countries hate Obama's militarism, 48–52
Arab countries hate Obama's weakness, 44–47
defined, 66
Europe will move toward, 53–58, 83
Europe will not move toward, 59–63
Islamic world dislikes US policies, 40–43
Latin America dislikes US policies, 64–75
political left hates US, 22–25
political right dishonors American values, 26–30
pop culture counteracts, 81–86
Russia dislikes US policies, 7–9
support for US is mixed, 10–11

the world hates US militarism, 10–21

Arab countries
hate US because of Obama's militarism, 48–52
hate US because of Obama's weakness, 44–47
Islamic world dislikes US policies, 31–43
See also specific countries

Arab Spring (2011), 63

Arafat, Yasser, 38

Argentina, anti-American populism, 66–68

Asia, anti-Americanism, 83

Assad, Bashar al-, 8

Aznar, Jose Maria, 23

B

Bard, Mitchell, 26–30

Barhom, Ashraf, 82

Berlusconi, Silvio, 63

bin Laden, Osama, 35, 37, 47

Bolivia, anti-American populism, 64–65, 71, 75

Braga, Alice, 82

Brazil, anti-American populism, 66–67

Britain. *See* United Kingdom (UK)

Bush, George W.
Arab world dislikes, 44–45, 48, 49
Europe dislikes, 53, 61–62
German newspapers criticized, 55, 56

Q

R

S

T